Praise for *False Premise, False Promise*

"There is no better authority on Medicare for All than Sally Pipes, who lived under Canada's government-run health care system and knows firsthand its failings. She brings facts and clear-eyed reality to the debate to show why centralized control over health care is so wrong for America while explaining a better path forward."

—GRACE-MARIE TURNER, president, Galen Institute

"As a former CEO of a successful company, I know how important competition is to ensuring a thriving and innovative industry. If government takes over our health care system—as Sally Pipes knows all too well—Americans can expect long waits, poor care, and higher taxes. This book presents not only the facts but also the human suffering of Canadians and others living under government-controlled health care. A must-read for those who want to stop single-payer health care from coming to America."

—ANDY PUZDER, former CEO of CKE Restaurants

"In her brilliant *False Premise, False Promise*, Sally Pipes dissects "Medicare for All," laying bare the defects of all the single-payer proposals hatched by the Left—including the horror of urgently needed but fatally delayed treatment as suffered by her mother in the Canadian system—and makes the compelling case for market-based health care as America's vitally required prescription."

—PETE WILSON, governor of California

"People say health care is complicated—not really. It's government that has made it so. And no one can sort through the morass of health care policy and present the issues with such stark clarity as Sally Pipes. In *False Premise, False Promise*, she exposes the financial and the human costs of a government-run health care system. Death and taxes may be certain, but not Medicare for All, thanks to this new book."

—DR. ARTHUR B. LAFFER, founder and chairman of Laffer Associates

"A highly readable, thoroughgoing, and devastating indictment of Medicare for All. Pipes makes the convincing case that such a single-payer scheme in America would have horrific consequences for the health of just about everyone. It would also kill innovation."

—STEVE FORBES, chairman and
editor-in-chief of Forbes Media

FALSE

PREMISE

FALSE

PROMISE

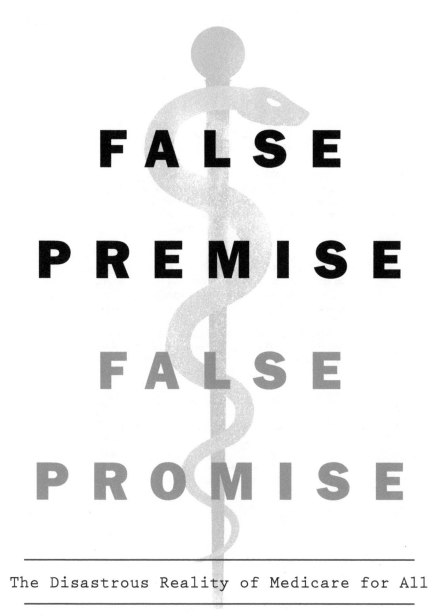

FALSE PREMISE

FALSE PROMISE

The Disastrous Reality of Medicare for All

SALLY C. PIPES

Encounter BOOKS

New York • London

First American edition published in 2020 by Encounter Books,
an activity of Encounter for Culture and Education, Inc.,
a nonprofit, tax-exempt corporation.
Encounter Books website address: www.encounterbooks.com

Manufactured in the United States and printed on
acid-free paper. The paper used in this publication meets
the minimum requirements of ANSI/NISO Z39.48-1992
(R 1997) (*Permanence of Paper*).

FIRST AMERICAN EDITION

LIBRARY OF CONGRESS CATALOGING-IN-PUBLICATION DATA
IS AVAILABLE

ISBN: 978-1-64177-072-9
EBOOK: 978-1-64177-073-6

CONTENTS

FOREWORD

American health care is at a crossroads.

The Affordable Care Act has failed to deliver on its promises. Five years after President Obama's signature legislative achievement went into full effect, individual market premiums have risen 75 percent.[1] Many low- and middle-income people have been forced into plans with deductibles as high as $12,000.[2]

Americans know the system is broken, and they're demanding change. Lawmakers know they can't sit idly by—they have to act.

Some progressives hope to use this public discontent to usher in something that would've been unthinkable less than a decade ago—a complete government takeover of the health care system.

"Medicare for All" seems simple enough on its face—enroll every American in Medicare, and have the federal government pick up the tab.

Unsurprisingly, many Americans are drawn to this plan. To hear Medicare for All's advocates tell it, it's easy to give every American high-quality care—we've just historically lacked the political will.

Of course, there's a lot these Medicare for All cheerleaders won't tell you.

They won't tell you that the existing Medicare program can barely stay afloat. It spent more than $50 billion on fraudulent payments in 2017, and its main hospital insurance trust fund is expected to go bankrupt by 2026.[3]

They won't tell you how they plan to cover the multi-trillion-dollar cost of giving every man, woman, and child "free" government-run health insurance.

And they won't tell you how government-run health systems have failed to provide quality care to patients—whether abroad in the United Kingdom and Canada or here at home in the Veterans Health Administration.

In *False Premise, False Promise*, Sally Pipes will tell you all of this and more.

This important book exposes the lies that supporters of Medicare for All love to tell. Their plan won't make Americans healthier, nor is it "free." Medicare for All won't reduce government spending, nor will it make our health care system more efficient.

This book also shows in startling detail what socialized medicine is like around the world: the long waits, shoddy care, and poor outcomes that patients living under government-run health systems must endure. And unlike Medicare for All's most strident supporters, Sally grounds her case against single-payer plans in facts and reason.

She doesn't just expose the false promise of Medicare for All. Sally refutes the great lie of socialism—the promise that a benevolent government can give people everything they want at no cost. This is the call of declining nations around the world, the tool of tyrants who use promises of equality to obstruct individual freedom.

But this book is more than a refutation of socialized medicine. It also charts a path forward. Sally shows how market forces can bring transparency, efficiency, and quality to health care, just as they do in every other sector of the economy. The key is less government intervention—not more.

This book is an excellent resource for any American who's concerned about their health, their family's health, and the health of our great nation. Whether you're a staunch supporter of Medicare for All, a fervent opponent, or on the fence, there's something for you in these pages.

—Tom Coburn, MD,
U.S. Senator, Oklahoma (Retired)

"MEDICARE FOR ALL" MANIA SWEEPS THE POLITICAL LEFT

The year is 2016. Senator Bernie Sanders has just lost the Democratic presidential primary to Hillary Clinton. He ran a fierce campaign, garnering more than 13 million votes—43 percent of the total cast.[1]

Sanders's long-term political legacy won't be his second-place finish in 2016. It will be his introduction of Medicare for All to the masses. "It is time for our country to join every other major industrialized nation on earth and guarantee health care to all citizens as a right, not a privilege," Sanders said upon releasing his vision for socialized medicine in the United States.[2]

For decades, Sanders has been advocating for a government health care monopoly. He envisioned a world where the federal government was the only provider of health coverage in the United States—where it was the "single payer" for health care.

Sanders had long been dismissed as an extremist, a self-proclaimed Democratic Socialist who honeymooned in the Soviet Union.[3] But after 2016, he couldn't be ignored any longer. Millions of people had thrown in their lot with a candidate who promised Medicare for All.

Perhaps that shouldn't have come as a surprise. Support for a single-payer system has grown steadily over the past two decades. Fifty-one percent of Americans favored single-payer health care in 2019, compared to just 40 percent in 2000, according to the Kaiser Family Foundation. As of the summer of 2019, 72 percent of Democrats were on board with Medicare for All.[4]

Democrats have scrambled to meet Sanders on their party's far left flank. When he introduced bills to establish Medicare for All in 2017 and then again in 2019, his legislation attracted more than a dozen Democratic cosponsors, including a host of presidential hopefuls.[5] Compare that to his earlier bids for single-payer legislation in the Senate—in 2009, 2011, and 2013—when he picked up nary a cosponsor.[6]

How did Medicare for All move from a fringe policy proposal to something that ostensibly commands the support of the majority of the American public? Like many radical political shifts, it's the product of years of dissatisfaction with the status quo.

A January 2019 Gallup poll found that 7 in 10 Americans believed the current health care system was "in a state of crisis" or had "major problems." That level of dissatisfaction has remained relatively constant since 1994, when Gallup first asked Americans how they felt about their country's health care system.[7]

By and large, it's the cost of care, not the quality, that's making Americans unhappy. In November 2018, more than half of Americans told Gallup they were satisfied with the quality of care they received.[8] Almost 80 percent said they were dissatisfied with its cost.[9]

It's easy to understand why. Health costs have been rising inexorably, much faster than the price of just about everything else in the economy. Between 2008 and 2018, the cost of health care in the United States increased nearly 22 percent. That's four percentage points higher than the overall inflation rate.[10]

Insurance premiums have grown even more. The average premium for employer-sponsored family coverage increased 54 percent between 2009 and 2018, to just over $20,000.[11] Nominal average wages have grown more slowly.[12] So health insurance costs are eating up a bigger and bigger share of Americans' paychecks.

The Affordable Care Act, signed into law by President Barack Obama on March 23, 2010, was supposed to address these trends. Its architects promised that its combination of mandates and subsidies would lower the cost of care and ensure no American went without coverage.

On both counts, the law, nicknamed Obamacare, failed. Average individual market premiums doubled between 2013—the year before most of Obamacare took effect—and 2017, according to the Department of Health and Human Services.[13]

About 20 million people gained insurance coverage through the Affordable Care Act.[14] But most of them ended up on Medicaid.[15] By 2018, around 27.5 million people were uninsured, according to the Census Bureau.[16] In 2019, 11.4 million people had coverage on either a state exchange or the federal government's HealthCare.gov. That year, 87 percent of those who shopped on the federal exchange received subsidies to purchase coverage.[17]

Obamacare's failure has provided an opening for politicians like Senator Sanders to call for even more government intervention in the health care marketplace. After all, Obamacare left private insurers intact. It gave them tens of billions of dollars in taxpayer-funded subsidies in hopes of making coverage more affordable. Yet insurance became even more expensive. Millions remain uninsured.

Sanders and company have framed this state of affairs as a failure of the private market—a failure only government can address. To make their case, Medicare for All's partisans point to the likes of Canada and the United Kingdom, whose government-run health care systems have furnished all citizens with insurance for a much smaller share of the national income.

There's just one problem. Government-run, single-payer health care is a catastrophe for the people forced to live under it. This book explains how and why.

In the following chapters, I'll tackle the big questions, like whether there is a "right" to health care. I'll survey the various single-payer proposals floating through the halls of Congress and detail how single-payer systems took root in Canada and the United Kingdom. I'll also lay out the horrors of those systems—from the unimaginably long waits for care and the lack of access to cutting-edge treatment to the eye-popping costs of "free" care and the subpar outcomes they deliver for patients.

Along the way, I'll introduce some of the victims of these systems: mothers denied lifesaving drugs for their children, young women told they aren't sick enough to qualify for care, and retirees heading abroad after being refused care at home, among others. Their stories should serve as cautionary tales for anyone who thinks a single-payer system is a good fit for the American people.

I'll then offer a health care reform plan of my own, one that will make affordable, quality care available to each and every American. Unlike Medicare for All, my plan doesn't double down on a half-century's worth of failed government overreach. Instead, it aims to unleash the market forces that have yielded higher quality, lower cost, and better value in every other sector of our economy. Only then will health care truly be affordable and accessible to all.

CHAPTER ONE

HEALTH CARE IS NOT A RIGHT

At its core, the case for single-payer health care rests on the assumption that wealthy nations can afford to guarantee a right to health care.

That seems simple enough. Who could oppose a societal effort to make sure everyone has access to health care?

A right to health care is not a new idea. In 1948, the United Nations unveiled the Universal Declaration of Human Rights. Article 25 of the declaration states, "Everyone has the right to a standard of living adequate for the health and well-being of himself and of his family, including... medical care."[1]

Throughout his nearly five-decades-long career, Senator Edward Kennedy argued for "decent quality health care as a fundamental right and not a privilege."[2] President Bill Clinton envisioned enshrining a new right to health care during his unsuccessful push for universal health care—dubbed "Hillarycare"—in the 1990s.[3]

In 2013, President Obama defended his eponymous 2010 health law by declaring, "In the United States, health care is not a privilege for the fortunate few, it is a right."[4] Democrats today, from Bernie Sanders on the left to the more centrist former vice president Joe

Biden, are carrying on that quest of guaranteeing a right to health care.[5]

This rhetoric presents a false choice. Health care is neither a right for the many nor a privilege for the few. It's a good and a service, just like everything else in our market economy.

SCARCITY CAN'T BE WISHED AWAY

Scarcity is one of the fundamental concepts of economics. Societies have limited resources. They have to be apportioned somehow. Tradeoffs are inevitable.

Establishing a right to health care creates the prospect of infinite demand for care. But health care goods and services are necessarily scarce. There's no way to create an unlimited supply to meet that potential demand.

Northwestern University professor Craig Garthwaite points out that health care is not a public good whose consumption the government can regulate, like parks or clean air. "If I consume health care services, someone else can't," he said in an interview with *Vox*.[6]

By dressing health care up in the language of rights, single-payer advocates are really calling for health care to be free at the point of access. Dr. Adam Gaffney, the president of Physicians for a National Health Program, has said that making people pay for health care "is just a way of punishing the sick and the poor." He points to the United Kingdom's National Health Service as proof that free health care is not simply "pie-in-the-sky and unrealistic."[7]

Economics is not a concern for those who maintain that there's an individual right to health care.

The National Economic and Social Rights Initiative (NESRI), for instance, gave Medicare for All "full marks for ... providing equal care to all residents regardless of immigration status, income, or past health record."[8] Conspicuously absent from its analysis was any discussion of how to pay for the plan. Ben Palmquist, NESRI's manager, told the *Nation* that "financing health care is a question of what we value as a country."[9]

Willing health care to be free is not a financing plan.

Let's set aside the practicalities of supply and demand for a moment. What would it actually mean to have a right to health care?

WHAT'S IN A RIGHT?

First, we must clarify what rights are. A right is something to which a person is morally and legally entitled. Broadly speaking, there are two types of rights.

Positive rights give us something and require someone else to give it to us. The right to health care would be a positive right. If the government is to enforce that right—to allow people to exercise it—then the government will have to be the one to directly provide or otherwise finance the provision of health care.

Negative rights require others to step aside and allow people to act independently. Most of the rights we hold dear as Americans are negative rights. Our government is built on the notion of negative liberty.

The Declaration of Independence states that everyone is "endowed by their Creator with certain unalienable Rights, that among these are Life, Liberty, and the pursuit of Happiness, [and] that to secure these rights, Governments are instituted among Men."[10]

Note what this means. Life, liberty, and the pursuit of happiness are not things a person can get from the government—they're things we're born with. Government exists to secure these rights, by establishing conditions that allow us to live freely.

Negative rights are also found in the Constitution. Take the First Amendment: "Congress shall make no law respecting an establishment of religion ... or abridging the freedom of speech."[11] Our rights to freedom of religion or speech don't come from government—government is simply prohibited from infringing upon them.

It is much easier to define and secure negative rights. It's what our government does best. Defining the criteria for positive rights, on the other hand, is tricky.

What does a right to health care guarantee? Is it just a right to free medical care?

Perhaps it's a right to quality medical care, or efficient medical care. If so, which tradeoffs are we willing to make? The government can provide shoddy medical care to a lot of people quickly and cheaply. But that's probably not what single-payer advocates have in mind.

Look at how many questions arise as we try to establish a baseline for what we mean by a right to health care. These difficulties are in part why we don't claim to have a "right" to other basic necessities.

Imagine the debate that would ensue over a "right to food." Does that mean a right not to go hungry? Maybe it's a right to consume the necessary number of calories each day. If so, does it matter where those calories come from? It's easier and cheaper to consume 2,000 calories at McDonald's than at a farmer's market. But that isn't the healthiest option. The questions and complications are overwhelming and don't come with easy answers.

Similarly, rights presuppose a level of equality that cannot be achieved in health care. We can't pay for a speedier trial or freer exercise of religion.

Does a right to health care entitle everyone to seek treatment from the best doctors or at the best hospitals? And to ensure equal protection of that right to health care, would the government have to ban people from paying extra for better treatment? Perhaps top-notch facilities would be prevented from offering innovative procedures—and instead compelled to offer a suite of government-sanctioned services.

This puts the government in a bind as well. If there's a $100,000 pill that can cure a group of patients, but the government can only afford to give it to half of them, what do we do?

In countries with single-payer programs, equality often takes precedence over health. Nobody would get that pill.

RIGHTS AND DUTIES

The right to health care may also push up against the rights of others. Negative rights basically require people to "live and let live."

Positive rights are more invasive. If everyone has a right to health care, the government could end up infringing on the rights of health care professionals. Can the government compel hospitals to take on more patients than they have beds to meet increased demand? Can it force doctors to log longer hours, work in subpar hospitals, or perform operations that go against their better judgment?

The right to health care would also impose duties on every citizen. The U.S. Supreme Court famously found that the right to free speech "would not protect a man in falsely shouting fire in a theatre and causing a panic."[12] Similarly, just because everyone has a right to travel does not mean they can careen down the interstate after consuming an entire bottle of scotch.[13]

If I have a right to health care, do I also have a duty to keep myself healthy? Do I waive my right to health care if I'm a smoker or if I'm obese? Would we be comfortable with the measures that officials in the United Kingdom have implemented to prohibit certain patients from having surgery unless they lose weight or quit smoking?[14]

Once the government is responsible for guaranteeing a right to health care, it has a plausible claim to micromanage what we eat, how much we exercise, and how we generally comport ourselves.

READY FOR A HEAVY DOSE OF PATERNALISM?

Universal health care is part of Canada's national identity. In 2012, a national poll found that 94 percent of Canadians felt their single-payer system was a "source of collective pride." Health care was more popular than hockey, the maple leaf flag, and the Queen.[15] In 2004, Canada's government-run broadcast service held a vote to determine the greatest Canadian. Canadians chose Tommy Douglas—the father of Canada's single-payer system.[16]

Americans would never take this much pride in a federal entitlement. There's a reason for this. Historically, Americans have given primacy to freedom over equality. To take just one piece of evidence for this statement, close to 6 in 10 Americans think "allowing everyone to pursue their life's goals without interference from the state" is more important than the state guaranteeing "nobody is in need," according to survey data from the Pew Research Center.[17]

This attitude is built into our national mythology and identity. It informed the American Revolution and the settlement of the American frontier. President Herbert Hoover called this attitude "rugged individualism."[18] Rugged individuals will always bristle at the idea of the government telling us what to do. We know that smoking is bad and eating vegetables is good, but we balk at the idea of public officials ordering us to do one and not the other.

Single-payer systems necessitate the kind of paternalism Americans have always rejected.

REGULATING OUR WAY TO HEALTH

As governments' health bills have skyrocketed, they've tried to intervene more and more in the daily lives of their citizens. The United Kingdom recently imposed "calorie caps" on fast food restaurants in an attempt to reduce national caloric intake.[19] The British government has also imposed a tax on companies that make sugary beverages, in hopes of forcing manufacturers to reduce the amount of sugar in their products.[20]

Several local governments in the United States have taken to nannying their residents for public health reasons. In 2014, Berkeley, California, imposed its own soda tax.[21] Chicago followed suit in August 2017; it repealed the tax just two months later after widespread protest from city residents.[22] In 2019, researchers found that Philadelphia's soda tax hadn't done much to decrease calorie or sugar intake.[23]

Alas, single-payer advocates rarely engage in these debates. Without a clear conception of what they mean by a right to health care, they forge ahead with plans that promise to pay for everything under the sun. Those promises are only revealed as empty when it's too late—when the financial realities of a single-payer system prevent the government from keeping its promises.

CHAPTER TWO

SINGLE-PAYER PROPOSALS UNDER CONSIDERATION

Advocates for single-payer health care have rolled out a number of plans for overhauling the U.S. health care system. The best-known, Medicare for All, would transform the system in less than five years. Others would install single-payer health care in slow motion, by offering more and more people the opportunity to "buy in" to Medicare, Medicaid, or a government-sponsored public health insurance option.

The pitch is seductive. Medicare for All and its more moderate alternatives make a lot of promises. If not "free" coverage, then few or no out-of-pocket costs. No insurance hassles. No more checking if a doctor is "in network." No referrals needed to see a specialist. No more worries about losing insurance because of unemployment.

But as the old saying goes, "If something sounds too good to be true, it probably is." That's certainly the case for Medicare for All.

THE SINGLE-PAYER "GOLD STANDARD"— MEDICARE FOR ALL

Bernie Sanders made Medicare for All part of the mainstream political vernacular during his 2016 presidential campaign. Washington Democrat Pramila Jayapal has taken up the baton in the House. She introduced her single-payer plan in February 2019.[1]

As of August 2019, more than a dozen Democratic senators had cosponsored Sanders's latest Medicare for All bid.[2] Jayapal's bill had more than 100 cosponsors.[3]

These bills have not yet been subject to analysis by the Congressional Budget Office (CBO) as of this writing. But on May 1, 2019, the nonpartisan agency did release a report analyzing the potential impact of single-payer plans more generally. The CBO concluded that government spending "would increase substantially under a single-payer system" while potentially leading "to lower quality of care for patients."[4]

That's an understatement. This grim forecast gets worse after diving into the specific plans under consideration.

COVERS EVERYTHING

Let's start with the plans' name, the misnomer "Medicare for All." The Sanders and Jayapal bills would actually destroy Medicare as we know it and dump all Americans—young and old, rich and poor—into a new government-run health plan.

Sanders and Jayapal promise soup-to-nuts coverage for everyone living in the United States, citizens and non-citizens alike. Their plans would cover hospital and physician care; chronic disease management; prescription drugs; medical devices; mental health and substance abuse treatment; laboratory and diagnostic services; reproductive services; maternity care; newborn care; pediatrics; long-term care; and even dental, vision, and hearing care.[5]

Not only would their plans cover everything imaginable—they'd do so free of charge. There would be no deductibles or coinsurance.

Sanders envisions a modest copay of up to $200 for prescription drugs; Jayapal eliminates even that.[6]

Patients could, in theory, see doctors on demand, with no referrals, preauthorizations, or provider networks. As Jayapal put it, "Patients will have complete freedom to choose the doctors, hospitals, and other providers they wish to see, without worrying about whether a provider is 'in-network.'"[7]

"Medicare for All" would be more generous than the existing Medicare program. Nearly one-third of the beneficiaries of traditional Medicare rely on current or former employers to supplement their coverage. Twenty-nine percent buy additional coverage on their own, on top of Medicare's baseline benefit. Twenty-two percent receive supplemental coverage from Medicaid.[8]

Those who do not have supplemental coverage under the existing Medicare program face the potential for unlimited out-of-pocket costs, a cap on the number of days they can spend in the hospital, and 20 percent coinsurance for outpatient care.[9]

By making care "free," Medicare for All would prompt unlimited demand from patients. But there's a limited supply of doctors, hospitals, and the like. Meeting that increase in demand would be impossible.

No other country in the world offers anything like what Sanders and Jayapal are proposing. Canada and the United Kingdom require some cost-sharing. Out-of-pocket costs—usually for things like prescription drugs—account for about 15 percent of national health expenditures in each country.[10] The same goes for Denmark, Norway, and Finland, where out-of-pocket spending accounts for 13.7 percent, 14.6 percent, and 20.4 percent of national health spending, respectively.[11]

THE END OF PRIVATE INSURANCE

Free, comprehensive health insurance, courtesy of the federal government. What's not to like? Plenty.

For starters, Medicare for All would outlaw private insurance coverage. As both the Sanders and Jayapal measures state, "It shall be unlawful for a private health insurer to sell health insurance coverage that duplicates the benefits provided under this Act." They'd also make it illegal for employers "to provide benefits for an employee, former employee, or the dependents of an employee or former employee that duplicate the benefits provided under this Act."[12]

So Medicare for All gives the government a monopoly over the provision of health insurance. And it forbids doctors who participate in the scheme from accepting private payment for any services the government covers.

In other words, it nationalizes the U.S. health insurance system.

Sanders and Jayapal counter that they'd permit the sale of private insurance for anything not covered by their Medicare for All plans. But the only things their plans don't cover are elective and cosmetic surgeries.

It's almost impossible, by definition, to buy insurance for elective procedures. Insurance is designed to help cover unexpected health costs. There's nothing unexpected about a nose job.

The level of disruption Medicare for All would unleash on the U.S. health care marketplace is breathtaking. The 181 million Americans who get health benefits through their jobs would be forced off their plans. So would the 52 million people who buy coverage on the individual market. The more than 20 million seniors with privately administered Medicare Advantage plans would lose their coverage.[13] Tens of millions of people are on managed care plans through Medicaid; they'd lose their coverage, too.[14]

Only those enrolled in the Veterans Health Administration and the Indian Health Service would be excluded from the Sanders-Jayapal vision for health reform. Of course, these two programs are pure manifestations of socialized medicine, as the government owns and operates hospitals and clinics directly. Not surprisingly, both are plagued by delays, poor-quality care, and rampant malfeasance.

Medicare for All's backers are convinced the public will love free health care so much they won't mind losing their private insurance. However, most people who say they support Medicare for All think they'll be able to keep their insurance.[15]

When the public learns that Medicare for All means outlawing private insurance, support collapses. (See vignette at end of chapter.)

A TRANSITION THAT OCCURS VIRTUALLY OVERNIGHT

Despite the challenges associated with shifting almost the entire population onto a new government-run insurance plan, both Sanders and Jayapal propose to implement Medicare for All in less than five years.

Sanders envisions a four-year transition. In year one, anyone younger than 19 or older than 55 would be enrolled in Medicare. In years two and three, anyone under 35 or older than 45 would be eligible. By year four, everyone in the country would have a "Universal Medicare" card.[16]

Jayapal hopes to accomplish the transition in just two years.[17] As the progressive news outlet Think Progress, which interviewed Jayapal and her staff, put it, "The thinking is that as the federal government radically reforms the system, insurance companies may exit existing marketplaces, leaving patients without plans or increasing premiums. This means a Medicare for All program would need to be implemented as quickly as possible."[18]

These timelines are beyond unrealistic. Democrats had three and a half years to build HealthCare.gov, the website for Obamacare's exchanges. It catered to a fraction of those who would be subject to Medicare for All. The website suffered a catastrophic meltdown when it officially opened for business in 2013. Just six people were able to sign up for coverage on HealthCare.gov's first day.[19]

Does the federal government really believe it can build an infrastructure to process all the country's health insurance claims, much less bring about the rest of Medicare for All's diktats, in less time than it took to build HealthCare.gov?

GLOBAL BUDGETS AND DRACONIAN
PRICE CONTROLS

Sanders and Jayapal propose to pay for their plan by ordering doctors, hospitals, and other health care providers to take massive pay cuts. Sanders would reimburse every health care provider at current Medicare rates.[20] Medicare pays hospitals 62 percent of what private insurance pays, while doctors collect 75 percent of private insurance rates.[21]

Jayapal's bill proposes a more extreme solution—global budgets. Providers would be paid a lump sum to be determined by the secretary of Health and Human Services. These payments would have to cover all medical services as well as staff salaries and administrative costs.[22]

The House bill would also require the government to set a cap for national health spending. This would limit how much could be spent nationwide each year for benefits, professional education, administrative costs, capital projects, and public-health activities.[23]

In addition, Jayapal and Sanders plan to impose price controls on pharmaceuticals. Sanders has claimed that price controls on prescription drugs could cut spending by almost one-third, saving up to $113 billion per year.[24]

In reality, such controls would hamper drug development. A study published in *Forum for Health Economics and Policy* found that implementing price controls solely in the existing Medicare Part D drug benefit would reduce "the number of new drug introductions by as much as 25 percent relative to the status quo."[25]

Another study, from the AEI-Brookings Joint Center for Regulatory Studies, looked at what would have happened had the country imposed comparatively modest price controls in the 1980s and 1990s. It found that there would have been "198 fewer new drugs brought to the U.S. market over this period." As a result, the authors concluded price controls "would have caused much more harm than good."[26]

A GARGANTUAN PRICE TAG

Medicare for All would be not just disruptive but expensive, too. A study by Charles Blahous, a scholar at the Mercatus Center, estimated that Medicare for All would add between $32.6 trillion and $38.8 trillion to the federal budget over its first 10 years. The total cost to the federal government could run between $54.6 trillion and $60.7 trillion over its first decade, according to Blahous.[27] Research from the left-leaning Urban Institute has arrived at similar numbers.[28]

It's hard to fathom how big those figures are. The entire federal government is on track to spend a grand total of $57.8 trillion over the next decade. That means Medicare for All would increase total federal spending by more than 55 percent.[29]

Even doubling individual and corporate federal income tax receipts would be insufficient to cover the cost of Medicare for All.[30] To finance his bill, Senator Sanders has floated several ideas, including a new 4 percent income tax for families, hikes in payroll and estate taxes, and new fees on major financial institutions.[31]

Sanders, Jayapal, and company are well aware of these estimates. That's why they haven't bothered to release detailed financing plans for their bills.

Instead, they claim that a 14-figure price tag is a deal. They say Medicare for All would reduce the country's health bill by $2 trillion over 10 years by empowering the government to drive a harder bargain with pharmaceutical companies and reduce administrative waste in our current multi-payer system.[32]

But the multitrillion-dollar estimates that Sanders and friends decry are almost certainly low. The Mercatus Center report, for example, gave Medicare for All the benefit of the doubt—and assumed its proposed payment cuts would go off without a hitch.

Blahous told the *Washington Post* that "to lend credibility to the $2 trillion savings number, one would have to argue that we can cut payments to providers by about 40 percent at the same time as increasing demand by about 11 percent."[33]

It's improbable that hospitals, doctors, and other providers would agree to do more work and receive less money in return. But that's the assumption behind Medicare for All.

The bill's purported administrative savings are unlikely to materialize, either. Cheerleaders for government-run care cite the current Medicare program's purportedly low administrative costs—just 1.1 percent of total spending in 2018.[34]

But that figure is misleading. For starters, other government agencies help administer Medicare. The IRS collects the taxes that fund it. The Department of Health and Human Services pitches in with office space and accounting help. The money those agencies spend helping Medicare doesn't appear on the program's balance sheet.

Second, Medicare's current beneficiaries are seniors and a small number of disabled individuals, who generally have much higher health costs than the general population. So by necessity the program devotes a much larger share of its expenses to medical claims than a private insurer with a person of average health might.

This reality doesn't tell us whether Medicare is more efficient than private insurers. It just reveals that the program spends a lot on medical care.

Third, Medicare is beset by fraud. In 2017, the agency made $52 billion in "improper payments."[35] That's about 7 percent of the program's total expenditures that year.[36] Reducing administrative costs is pointless if it allows health care providers to submit fraudulent claims with impunity.

In addition, many of Medicare for All's supposed administrative "savings" will simply be offloaded onto providers.[37] Hospitals today spend close to $40 billion a year complying with federal rules and regulations. In 2016 alone, the federal government produced nearly 24,000 pages of regulations governing hospitals and acute care providers.[38]

Medicare for All would require providers to regularly submit reams of additional data to the feds, including "annual financial data, the number of registered nurses per staffed bed, and spending on health IT."[39]

Then there are the costs associated with the destruction of the private health insurance sector. Jayapal acknowledges that about 1 million people who currently work in the insurance industry could lose their jobs.[40] She proposes setting aside up to 1 percent of her national health budget to assist these workers.[41] That's billions of taxpayer dollars. Further, the government would have to hire scores of employees to run Medicare for All.

Finally, single-payer health care's advocates ignore the ugly fiscal history of federal health care programs.

Medicare suffered massive cost overruns almost as soon as it launched in 1965.[42] Hospital costs increased 21.9 percent in the program's first year and continued to grow an average of 14 percent in each of the next five years.[43] Two years after Medicare opened for business, President Lyndon Johnson had to promise in his State of the Union address that he'd tackle runaway medical price inflation.[44]

When Medicare added dialysis coverage in 1972, it was supposed to cover 16,000 seniors and cost just $209 million by 1976.[45] The actual cost was more than twice that. Within a decade, the price tag for this one benefit had exploded to nearly $2 billion. By 1992, it topped $6 billion.[46]

In 1965, the House Ways and Means Committee projected that Medicare's Part A hospital insurance program would run about $9 billion a year by 1990. The actual cost was more than seven times that figure—$67 billion. According to a 2009 report from the Senate Joint Economic Committee, the actuary who came up with those estimates said Part A spending was 165 percent higher than his estimate, even after taking into account the high inflation of the 1970s.[47]

In 1972, Congress passed its first Medicare cost-control bill. During the 1980s, lawmakers enacted price controls for hospitals and doctors. In the late 1990s, they passed another round of cost-cutting measures for the program.[48] Even Obamacare tried to squeeze hundreds of billions out of Medicare. Nothing has worked.

In 2019, the Board of Trustees for Medicare and Social Security predicted that unless drastic measures were taken, Medicare's hospital insurance fund, Part A, would run consistent multibillion-dollar annual deficits before going bankrupt in 2026.[49]

Medicaid's costs have ballooned in much the same way. According to a 1969 Senate Finance Committee report, "Expenditures under the Medicaid program have increased much more rapidly than anyone had anticipated. Between 1965 and 1970, total Federal, State, and local costs rose from $1.3 billion to $5.5 billion."[50]

A 2016 report found that Medicaid costs in the District of Columbia and the 36 states that expanded the program under Obamacare were 49 percent higher in 2015 than expected.[51]

To say Medicare for All will more than pay for itself is a fantasy of the first order.

THE SINGLE-PAYER-IN-SLOW-MOTION SCHEMES

Some of the more moderate Democrats are worried that the public will object to the rapid transformation of the health care system that Medicare for All would bring about. In an interview with *Rolling Stone*, House Speaker Nancy Pelosi offered up the question many rank-and-file Democrats are afraid to ask: "How do you pay for that?"[52]

Moderate Democrats have been pushing supposedly incremental alternatives, like government-sponsored insurance plans or schemes that grant those not currently eligible for Medicare or Medicaid the ability to "buy in" to the programs.

As of this writing, there were half a dozen such proposals at the federal level. A closer look reveals that they're just attempts to deliver single-payer care on the installment plan.

MEDICARE AT 50

Michigan senator Debbie Stabenow describes her "Medicare at 50" bill as a prudent and cost-effective way to expand affordable coverage. Unlike Medicare for All, she says, it could "be implemented right away . . . and has a lot of support and enthusiasm in the country."[53]

A number of her colleagues agree. Twenty fellow Democrats have signed on as cosponsors.[54]

Stabenow's plan would let anyone 50 or older purchase Medicare coverage at a government-set premium. Anyone who bought in would receive coverage for hospital care, physician care, and prescription drugs, just like seniors who are currently enrolled. People would even have the option to enroll in privately administered Medicare Advantage plans, which offer a mixture of Medicare's traditional benefits and some not covered by the legacy program, like vision or dental care.

Because enrollees would be responsible for their own premiums, Stabenow says, her plan wouldn't cost taxpayers a dime. Premiums would go into a Medicare Buy-In Trust Fund, which would supposedly cover the cost of care for these new enrollees.

Stabenow's plan would also let Medicare "negotiate fair prices" for prescription drugs. Negotiations with an actor the size of the federal government are hardly negotiations—they're price controls by a different name.

Whatever Stabenow claims about the reasonableness of her bill, it's just another route to single-payer health care. If "Medicare at 50" were to become law, Congress would face immediate pressure to lower the eligibility age. Stabenow herself has already bowed to this pressure. "Medicare at 50" is an updated version of a "Medicare at 55" bill she introduced in 2017.[55]

Since Medicare could rely on price controls to keep its costs down, it would soon be able to underprice all the private plans for sale on the exchanges. Soon, a Medicare plan would be the only "option" left.

MEDICARE FOR AMERICA

Another bill that would drive the country toward a single-payer plan is Medicare for America. Introduced on May 1, 2019, and sponsored by Representatives Rosa DeLauro (D-CT) and Jan Schakowsky (D-IL), this bill is essentially one step shy of Medicare for All.

The measure would overhaul Medicare to cover more benefits, including dental and vision care. Anyone could buy into the new program. Premiums would be capped at 9.69 percent of income. Those with incomes between 200 percent and 600 percent of the poverty level would get premium subsidies; those below 200 percent would pay nothing.[56]

Like every other Democratic health care plan, Medicare for America would impose price controls on prescription drugs. Specifically, it would allow the government to "negotiate" prices "based on value assessments." If negotiations failed, the government could simply adopt the Veterans Affairs' price controls or tie the drug's price to the average paid by countries with price controls on drugs.[57]

Unlike Medicare for All, Medicare for America includes some cost-sharing, with deductibles of $350 for individuals and $500 for families, as well as annual out-of-pocket maximums of $3,500 and $5,000. Medicare for America would also leave Medicare Advantage untouched and allow businesses to provide benefits for workers.

"There are 160 million people who get their insurance through their employer," DeLauro told the *Huffington Post*. "You cannot tell them overnight that it is gone."[58]

Not overnight, perhaps. But under Medicare for America, those employer plans wouldn't last long. That's because Medicare for America would require employers to offer gold-plated insurance equivalent to the revamped Medicare.[59] That mandate would prove prohibitively costly for scores of employers.

Medicare for America anticipates as much—and so allows employers to pay an 8 percent payroll tax to move their workers onto the new government-run plan.[60] For many employers, an 8 percent payroll tax would be preferable to the headache of managing a benefits program. The private employer-sponsored insurance market would gradually wither away.

Medicare for America's premiums wouldn't be enough to pay for the program. Its creators offer a host of taxes to fill the gap: a rollback of the 2017 federal income tax cuts, new taxes on the rich, increases in the existing Medicare payroll tax, and regressive tax hikes on beer, wine, liquor, soft drinks, and cigarettes.[61]

MEDICARE-X CHOICE ACT

In April 2019, Senator Michael Bennet (D-CO) and 11 cosponsors introduced the Medicare-X Choice Act.[62] A similar measure introduced in the House by Representative Antonio Delgado (D-NY) had 19 cosponsors, as of September 2019.[63] The bills would essentially create a federally chartered health plan available to everyone who purchases coverage through Obamacare's exchanges.

Initially, only those who live in areas with one option or no options on their exchange or in counties where a shortage of health providers or lack of competition results in exorbitant costs could buy into the plan. But within three years, Medicare would be an option for every individual buying coverage through an Obamacare exchange. A year after that, it would be open for every small business on Obamacare's SHOP exchanges.[64]

The new health plan's benefits would be the same as other plans in the Obamacare exchanges, and premiums would cover the bill's entire cost. The legacy Medicare program would remain the same.[65]

Medicare-X is, in short, the public option liberal Democrats pushed for—and moderate Senate Democrats killed—during the debate over Obamacare. Former vice president Joe Biden is among the most prominent supporters of a public option, if not Medicare-X Choice explicitly.[66]

In a postmortem on the public option, one of its progenitors called it "a voluntary transition toward single-payer insurance."[67]

Unburdened by the need to cover its costs, the government would be able to set premiums under Medicare-X Choice lower than its private competitors. Those private plans would exit the market in short order; eventually, the public option would be the only option left.

CHOOSE MEDICARE ACT

Fourteen senators have cosponsored Oregon Democrat Senator Jeff Merkley's Choose Medicare Act.[68] This plan would add one more letter to Medicare's alphabet—Medicare Part E.

Anyone shopping on Obamacare's exchanges could enroll in Part E. Additionally, employers of all sizes could choose to enroll their workers in Part E instead of offering a private plan.[69] At the same time, the bill would expand Obamacare's costly rate and benefit mandates to employer plans that are currently exempt from them in order to "level the playing field."[70]

Part E would cover all of Obamacare's "essential health benefits," along with "all items and services covered by Medicare." It would also cap out-of-pocket spending in the traditional Medicare program.[71]

Senator Merkley said, "The Choose Medicare Act creates a Medicare option for all, putting consumers and businesses in the driver's seat on the pathway to universal health care."[72]

As with all other buy-in schemes, however, the ultimate goal of the Choose Medicare Act is to destabilize the employer and individual markets until Medicare is the only game in town. Senator Merkley has admitted as much: "If we could make the leap straight to 'Medicare for all,' I would love for us to do that. But it's important to lay out a route about how we get to that vision."[73]

MEDICAID BUY-IN

Democrats are also looking to Medicaid as a potential path to single-payer insurance. Obamacare took a huge step in this direction by enticing most states to expand eligibility to those making up to 138 percent of the federal poverty level, including able-bodied, childless adults.

Several Democrats in Congress and more than a dozen states are considering letting even more people buy into it.[74] The new enrollees would be responsible for the full cost of coverage. That cost is unlikely to be high, given that Medicaid's reimbursement rates are much lower than those for Medicare or private insurance.

In early 2019, Senator Brian Schatz (D-HI) and Representative Ben Ray Lujan (D-NM) introduced the State Public Option Act to "create a Medicaid-based public health care option to strengthen the Affordable Care Act by providing Americans with a new high-quality, low-cost choice when purchasing health insurance."[75] The bill would allow states to create Medicaid buy-in programs for all their residents, regardless of income. Premiums would be capped at 9.5 percent of family income.[76]

MEDICARE EXTRA FOR ALL

In addition to all these legislative offerings, liberal think tanks are developing their own single-payer plans.

Take the left-wing Center for American Progress's "Medicare Extra for All." The plan is similar to Medicare for America—but more expansive. Everyone would be eligible to enroll in Medicare Extra, including those already on Medicare, veterans, and federal employees.[77]

After the plan went into effect, newborns and anyone over the age of 65 would be automatically enrolled.[78] Like Medicare for All, it would cover just about every conceivable health care service, from surgery and drugs to dental and vision care.[79]

Medicare Extra would abolish premiums for families with incomes up to 150 percent of the poverty line. Premiums would be capped at 10 percent of income for those who make more than five times the poverty rate. Deductibles, copayments, and out-of-pocket limits would also vary by income.[80]

As with Medicare for All, the plan would ban private insurance from providing coverage that duplicates Medicare Extra's benefits. Medicare Advantage would get revamped as well.[81]

Initially, employer-sponsored insurance would survive. However, employers would have the option of enrolling their employees in Medicare Extra. Individuals whose employers provided private insurance would also be able to enroll in Medicare Extra on their own. Employers would pay the same amount toward premiums, while the employee share would be capped.[82]

STATE-LEVEL SINGLE-PAYER PLANS

Several states are not waiting for the federal government to take action. They're considering single-payer systems of their own.

California's move toward single-payer health care appears to be on hold. In 2017, the state senate ratified a bill that would put all Californians into a government-run health plan.[83] But the measure stalled in the state assembly and has been on ice ever since.

Governor Gavin Newsom has been a longtime supporter of single-payer systems. But it's unlikely that the idea will get off the ground any time soon. An analysis by the state Legislative Analyst's Office pegged the annual cost of single-payer care at $400 billion, double the total state budget.[84]

Single-payer advocates in New York have run into similar delays. The state assembly approved a bill establishing single-payer health care in New York in 2018 for the fourth consecutive year, only to see it idle in the state senate.[85]

In 2019, Democrats took both chambers of the state legislature and retained control of the governorship. But cost has remained a major impediment to passage of the plan. The RAND Corporation estimated that a single-payer system would require $139 billion in new state tax revenue by 2022.[86]

In March 2019, the authors of the New York Health Act, State Assemblyman Richard Gottfried and Senator Ricardo Rivera, added coverage for long-term care to their bill.[87] That would increase its cost by $18 billion to $20 billion, bringing the total to $160 billion. That's well over double what the state currently collects in taxes.[88]

Some portions of the Democratic political coalition have balked at New York's single-payer plan. Several key labor unions worry that single-payer health care would lead to worse health benefits for their members—at greater cost.[89] Governor Andrew Cuomo has withheld his support, too, claiming that single-payer systems should be dealt with at the federal level.[90]

Colorado and Washington have opted for the public option. In late April 2019, the Colorado legislature approved a bill that directed two state agencies to come up with a plan, including information on costs, funding, what the federal government would need to approve and fund, eligibility, and who would administer the program. Governor Jared Polis signed the bill into law in May 2019.[91] Absent any hiccups, the plan could open for enrollment in late 2020.[92]

On May 13, 2019, Washington governor Jay Inslee signed a measure into law that directed the state to contract with one or more private insurance companies to create new health plans offering three different levels of benefits to sell on the state's insurance exchange. The state would dictate the terms of the plans and would set reimbursement rates at no more than 160 percent of what Medicare pays. The insurers would be responsible for signing up customers and processing claims. The state envisions the plans launching in 2021.[93]

THE MANY WAYS TO GOVERNMENT-RUN HEALTH CARE

Lawmakers claim Medicare and Medicaid buy-ins are reasonable ways to help people access affordable care without causing too much disruption to the status quo. In reality, these plans would devastate the nation's health care system—just more slowly than Medicare for All.

There's more than one way to bring about a government takeover of the health care system. Many of these plans may seem pie-in-the-sky—unlikely to come about.

That's what people in Canada and the United Kingdom thought decades ago, before their single-payer systems took root. Let's take a look at the disastrous history of single-payer systems in those two countries, in hopes that we might avoid repeating their mistakes in the United States.

Misleading Polls About Support for Medicare for All

Medicare for All's proponents claim they have the public on their side, and the polls seem to confirm as much. A July 2019 Kaiser Family Foundation survey found that 50 percent of people supported "having a national health plan, sometimes called Medicare for All."[94]

Medicare and Medicaid buy-in schemes also poll well. In that same Kaiser survey, more than three-quarters of the public said they supported Medicare at 50, including 69 percent of Republicans. Seventy-five percent said they backed a Medicaid buy-in.[95]

These polls just reveal that people respond favorably when they're offered something valuable for free.

But people don't understand what Medicare for All would entail. Seven in 10 Democrats think people with employer-sponsored insurance will be able to keep it under Medicare for All, according to a June 2019 Kaiser Family Foundation poll. Two-thirds of Democrats believe that people who purchase insurance on their own will be able to hold on to it under single-payer plans.[96]

When they learn about what it will take to bring about Medicare for All, or any of its single-payer cousins, their support vanishes.

Kaiser found that just 37 percent supported Medicare for All when told it would "eliminate private health insurance companies." Likewise, 37 percent were behind the idea when told it would "require most Americans to pay more in taxes." Tell people that a Medicare for All scheme would "lead to delays in people getting some medical tests and treatments," and support plunges to 26 percent.[97]

CHAPTER THREE

THE MARCH TO A
SINGLE-PAYER PLAN

It's tempting to brush off the Left's plans for single-payer health care as little more than political fantasy.

Yet the unworkability of single-payer plans is no bulwark against their implementation. Look no further than their history in Canada and the United Kingdom.

During the twentieth century, both places saw nationwide single-payer go from a vague idea to a concrete reality in a few short years. What followed was an unmitigated disaster: rampant rationing, exorbitant wait times, and care of embarrassingly poor quality.

So it's hardly unprecedented for a wealthy Western democracy to rush into a half-baked plan for socializing its health care system. Here's how both Canada and the United Kingdom made their leaps into the single-payer abyss.

CANADA'S SHORT ROAD TO LONG WAITS

Canada's single-payer system, known as Medicare, has its roots in a program spearheaded by Tommy Douglas, the premier of

Saskatchewan during the 1940s.[1] Douglas, a Scottish immigrant, was Canada's first premier from the Co-operative Commonwealth Federation (CCF), a socialist political party founded during the Great Depression.[2]

He established an ambitious system of government-funded hospital insurance to cover all residents of the province in 1947.[3] By 1961, an effort to expand the program to include visits to doctors' offices and clinics was under way—but not without controversy.[4]

The most notable opponents of the expansion were Saskatchewan's doctors. They were concerned that the new system of socialized medicine would drag down the quality of care. Physicians feared the program would give the province too much power to determine how patients were cared for—that it would relegate them to mere government functionaries.[5]

The doctors earned the backing of Saskatchewan's center-left Liberal Party, but their pleas ultimately went unheeded. The government adopted the expanded insurance scheme in 1961.

Physicians, however, didn't give up their fight. When the program launched in July 1962, most of the province's doctors went on strike. Twenty-three days later, they admitted defeat. Saskatchewan's government-run health insurance plan—the first single-payer system in North America—was the law of the land.[6]

At the time, few would have guessed that Saskatchewan's controversial experiment in socialized medicine would become national policy. Just four and a half years later, that's exactly what happened.

As in the United States, the 1960s were characterized by a leftward shift in the Canadian body politic. Left-leaning politicians were happy to capitalize on that shift—and make government-run health care a national priority.[7]

The pro-single-payer case was strengthened by the recommendations of the Royal Commission on Health Services, chaired by Justice Emmett Hall, a member of the center-right Conservative Party. In a landmark 1964 report, the commission endorsed a universal, single-payer system.[8]

The end result was the 1966 adoption of the Medical Care Act under Liberal prime minister Lester B. Pearson, which created a nationwide single-payer system. It passed the House of Commons by a sweeping 177–2 margin.[9]

It wasn't until 1984, and the passage of the Canada Health Act, that the country's single-payer system assumed its current form. The act put individual provinces and territories in charge of their own government-run health insurance plans. Canada's 13 provinces and territories must adhere to five criteria in order to receive their full share of federal health care funding.

First, each insurance plan must be a nonprofit operation run by a public authority. Second, plans must cover all medically necessary services provided by a physician or hospital. Third, provinces must give all insured individuals uniform access to covered treatments and services. Fourth, a resident who moves from one province to another must be covered by his original "home" province for a specified period of time, after which the new province must take over coverage. And fifth, all covered individuals must have reasonable access to care.[10]

The Canada Health Act gives provincial governments a monopoly over the provision of health insurance for anything deemed "medically necessary." Doctors and hospitals can operate independent of the government. But because private insurance coverage is more or less illegal, doctors and hospitals effectively have one paying customer—the government.

The stated purpose of the act was "to protect, promote and restore the physical and mental well-being of residents of Canada and to facilitate reasonable access to health services without financial or other barriers."[11] Unfortunately, the health care system created by the Canada Health Act has consistently fallen short of that goal by, for instance, forcing patients to endure lengthy waits for medically necessary treatments and procedures. In many cases, the failures of Canada's single-payer system have amounted to nothing less than an abrogation of Canadians' fundamental human rights.

"Canadian Health Care's Lack of Compassion Hits One Cancer-Stricken Family Hard"

Anya Humphrey of Campden, Ontario, knows more about palliative care than anyone should have to. In 2008, her husband Fred died of colon cancer. Four years later, her son Ted died of testicular cancer.[12]

In both instances, the Canadian health care system let her down. The elder Humphrey was sick for two years before he began receiving end-of-life care.[13] The care he ultimately received, just three weeks before he died, was an unfortunate combination of bureaucracy and mismanagement.[14]

The day after Mr. Humphrey met his care team, he had a "pain crisis."[15] His wife called the care team leader, who subsequently arranged a conference call with Telehealth Ontario, a government hotline that connects patients to registered nurses 24/7.[16] The care team leader "didn't have any idea how to manage" Mr. Humphrey's pain.[17] Mrs. Humphrey recalls her husband being "so disgusted that he...said he would rather just suffer" than keep dealing with his care team.[18]

Mrs. Humphrey's final assessment of her husband's palliative care is damning: "Fred's death was not peaceful and they were not here to support us and that was simply awful."[19]

When her son got sick, things were slightly different. "Nobody ever talked about palliative care with Ted because they really didn't think he was going to die," even though his cancer had spread throughout his body, Mrs. Humphrey told the Canadian Institute for Health Information. "He went through hell with chemo," she said. Ted Humphrey's experience with palliative care—or the lack thereof—"was just a nightmare."[20]

The Humphreys were one of the few families to receive any palliative care at all. A 2018 report from the Canadian Institute for Health Information found that fewer than one in six people received palliative home care in 2016–2017.[21]

"The system is simply not ready to give adequate support to everybody who wants to die at home," Mrs. Humphrey said.[22] She now advocates for improved access to quality palliative care so that fewer Canadians have to endure struggles like hers.

This was made clear with the Supreme Court of Canada's landmark decision in *Chaoulli v. Quebec.* At issue were several Quebec statutes prohibiting patients from purchasing private insurance for treatments and services already covered by the Canada Health Act.

George Zeliotis, a retired chemical salesman from Anjou, Quebec, had been waiting over a year for a hip replacement when he decided to do something about it.[23] Along with his physician, Dr. Jacques Chaoulli, Zeliotis challenged Quebec's ban on private coverage.[24]

Chaoulli and Zeliotis launched their suit in 1997. They claimed that, by banning patients from purchasing private coverage and thereby forcing them to wait for necessary treatment, the provincial government was violating fundamental protections included in both the Canadian Charter of Rights and Freedoms and the Quebec Charter of Human Rights and Freedoms. They kept up their fight over the next seven years, as first the Quebec Superior Court and then the Quebec Court of Appeal upheld the ban on private insurance.[25]

Finally, in June 2005, the Supreme Court of Canada ruled in favor of Chaoulli and Zeliotis.[26] In a 4–3 decision, the court ruled that the province's prohibition on private insurance did indeed violate the Quebec Charter's guaranteed "right to life, and to personal security, inviolability and freedom." But on the question of whether the law infringed on rights set down in the Canadian Charter, the court split 3–3.[27]

Chief Justice Beverley McLachlin summed up the position of the court in her majority opinion, writing, "Access to a waiting list is not access to health care."[28]

While the *Chaoulli* decision was confined to Quebec, it had significant national implications. It was an admission by Canada's highest court that laws aimed at propping up the government's health care monopoly actually abridged the basic freedoms of Canadians.

There is no shortage of lessons to draw from Canada's fraught history with single-payer health care, but one in particular deserves special attention. Once an idea like socialized medicine captures a nation's political imagination, it doesn't take long to become full-blown policy.

RISE OF THE NHS: ONE EMERGENCY
AFTER ANOTHER

The origins of the United Kingdom's single-payer system, the National Health Service (NHS), are equally informative. Officially founded in 1948, the program presently comprises four entities—one for each member of the United Kingdom. The vast majority of funding comes from general taxation as well as additional taxes known as "national insurance contributions."[29] The NHS charges nothing at the point of care for covered treatments, services, and procedures, with certain exceptions, including dental care, prescription drugs, and optical care.[30]

While government-funded health care had existed in some form for centuries in England, an early incarnation of the NHS dates to 1938. It was then, in the run-up to the Second World War, that the British government created what came to be known as the Emergency Hospital Service—later renamed the Emergency Medical Service.

This initiative consolidated the nation's hospitals into a single entity with the goal of freeing up capacity for war-related injuries.[31] The organization often struggled to distribute resources effectively between ordinary patients and war casualties. Many Britons found it difficult to get care.[32]

In principle, the Ministry of Health had the authority to dictate the policies of the nation's hospitals, which, at the time, were run by either local authorities or charities.[33] In reality, the hospitals that made up the Emergency Medical Service still enjoyed a great deal of autonomy during the war.[34] Nevertheless, the very existence of such a program helped normalize the idea of a government-run health sector in the United Kingdom.

Another turning point came in November 1942, when economist

Sir William Beveridge presented Parliament with a report entitled *Social Insurance and Allied Services*. The Beveridge Report, as it came to be known, outlined an ambitious vision for a modernized British welfare state.

Specifically, the document identified five "Giant Evils" the British government should set out to slay: "Want, Disease, Ignorance, Squalor, and Idleness." One of Beveridge's core proposals was that "medical treatment covering all requirements will be provided for all citizens by a national health service."[35]

The Labour Party under Prime Minister Clement Attlee set about implementing many of Beveridge's recommendations, following its victory in 1945 over Winston Churchill's Conservatives. That included the economist's vision for a government-run health service.[36]

As in Canada, the nation's doctors were less than enthusiastic about a government takeover of the health care system. The British Medical Association threatened a physician boycott if Health Minister Aneurin "Nye" Bevan moved ahead with the NHS.

To appease doctors concerned about their independence under a socialized system, Bevan made several substantive changes. For instance, hospitals would be overseen by regional boards, and physicians would be allowed to work in private practice on a part-time basis.[37]

It only took until July 5, 1948—less than six years after Beveridge's proposal—for the NHS to formally launch. The organization had three main branches. First was a system of 2,751 state-owned, locally run hospitals. Britain at that time had a total of 3,000 hospitals.[38] On top of that was a network of general practitioners paid set fees by the government. The third branch included facilities such as nursing homes and public-health organizations, which were operated by locally elected councils or authorities.[39]

From its inception, the NHS has struggled to accommodate patient demand. The government has rolled out one reform initiative after another. The most significant came in 1991, when Prime Minister Margaret Thatcher ushered in what was dubbed an "internal market" model. Under this new approach, the NHS was no longer administered by a single bureaucracy. Instead, the system was divided between purchasers—that is, government health authorities—and providers, which today are the hospitals and medical facilities known as NHS trusts.[40]

This reform effort did little to relieve the inefficiencies, lengthy delays for treatment, and financial problems that had plagued the NHS. So in 1999, the Labour government established a body that would more or less explicitly ration care to rein in patient demand—the National Institute for Clinical Excellence, or NICE.

"NHS: Sorry, You're Not Skinny Enough to Have an Eating Disorder"

Hope Virgo, a native of Bristol, England, developed anorexia when she was 12 years old.[41] "I had struggled with feelings of guilt and sadness for so long but from the day I met anorexia I discovered this amazing sense of relief," she told Wales Online.[42]

For four years, Virgo avoided food. She forced herself to vomit when she did eat and exercised furiously to keep her weight down. Just weeks after her family confronted her about her illness, she was admitted to the hospital with her "heart failing and [her] hair falling out."[43]

After a year working with mental health professionals, Virgo had managed to keep her anorexia at bay.[44]

But eating disorders aren't easily defeated. One study found that 30 percent of anorexia patients relapse after receiving treatment.[45] In 2017, at the age of 26, Virgo felt herself relapsing.[46]

When she sought help from her physician, the response shocked her. She was not skinny enough to qualify for anorexia treatment.[47] Specifically, she was told that her body mass index did not fall outside the range deemed healthy by the NHS.[48]

Virgo described spending the next month feeling like a "fake anorexic person who was not good at having an eating disorder."[49]

The National Institute for Health and Care Excellence, or NICE, estimates that more than 260,000 people over the age of 16 in the United Kingdom suffer from anorexia.[50] According to Rebecca Willgress, who runs communications at Beat, a U.K. charity dedicated to helping people with eating disorders, many patients share Virgo's experience.[51]

Willgress told Mashable, an online news outlet, that Beat hotline operators "often speak to people who were not referred for treatment because [they] were told their weight 'wasn't low enough,' which only deals another blow to their self-esteem and makes the situation worse."[52]

NICE guidelines instruct physicians to "not use single measures such as BMI...to determine whether to offer treatment for an eating disorder."[53] Clearly, that message isn't getting through to NHS doctors.

Virgo's encounter with the NHS inspired her to launch the #DumpTheScales campaign in July 2018 to encourage the government to review how it diagnoses and treats eating disorders.[54]

Virgo believes change is needed "to prevent people [from] getting more unwell, save the NHS money, and save lives." As of September 2019, her petition had received over 94,000 signatures.[55] #DumpTheScales has been debated in Parliament and acknowledged by Downing Street.[56]

———————————————

The body, later renamed the National Institute for Health and Care Excellence, is charged with evaluating treatments in order to establish uniform standards of care throughout the NHS.[57] In practice, however, NICE attempts to determine the clinical and cost-effectiveness of drugs and procedures in order to dictate whether they're worth paying for. Especially costly drugs or treatments which fail to extend life sufficiently, at least in NICE's estimation, are made off-limits for NHS patients.

Despite these challenges, the NHS lumbers on, generating a seemingly endless succession of scandals and atrocities. In this way, a government-run health care program hastily founded during a time of crisis has, more than seven decades later, become its own national emergency.

CHAPTER FOUR

THE HORRORS OF SINGLE-PAYER INSURANCE—WAITS

Single-payer systems have the impossible task of treating a constant flow of patients with finite resources. When demand for health care outstrips supply, single-payer administrators must resort to rationing or denying care.

Remember the bread lines during the Great Depression, or cars lining up for gas during the 1970s oil embargo? Single-payer health care brings those waits to hospitals, doctors' offices, and clinics.

GET IN LINE

Canadians may be known for their kindness and politeness, but even the gentlest Canuck is bound to get sick of my native country's health care system. Its delays for care would be laughable if they didn't leave millions of people in pain and suffering.

Since 1993, the Vancouver-based Fraser Institute has published *Waiting Your Turn*, an annual report examining wait times for health care in Canada. Those waits have headed in one direction over the past quarter-century—up.

The report chronicles two types of waits. The first is how long a patient waits between referral by a general practitioner to a specialist and consultation with that specialist. The second is how long the patient waits for treatment after consultation with a specialist. Together, these two metrics constitute "total wait time."[1]

Nationwide, the median total wait time was just under 20 weeks in 2018.[2] That's more than double the wait Canadian patients faced in 1993.[3]

Patients in New Brunswick, one of the Maritime provinces, fared the worst, waiting a median of 45 weeks between their initial appointments with general practitioners and specialist treatment.[4] Not far behind was Nova Scotia, where patients waited more than 34 weeks.[5]

In 2018, 72 percent of wait times nationwide exceeded what physicians would deem "reasonable."[6]

Only the sickest patients come close to securing relatively timely care. Cancer patients had the shortest total wait time in 2018—just four weeks. On the flip side, the median wait for orthopedic surgery was 39 weeks.[7]

These waits are particularly hard on elderly Canadians. Thirty percent of patients waited more than six months for hip and knee replacements in 2018.[8] One in five Canadians 55 and older says they have major issues accessing health care.[9]

In 2019, Vancouver retiree Jenny MacKenzie was told she would have to wait a full year for hip surgery, according to reporting from Canadian think tank SecondStreet.org. She was dealing with more than physical pain. "It really upsets me I can't cuddle my grandchildren or pick them up," MacKenzie said.[10]

All told, Canadians were waiting for nearly 1.1 million procedures in 2018. That means nearly 3 percent of the population were on a waiting list, if we assume one patient per procedure.[11] Extrapolate those numbers to the United States, and that's the equivalent of more than 9.8 million Americans waiting for care.[12]

"Sorry, Sir, There's No Room in Our Hospital"

Mary Louise Murphy was "sweating profusely and had trouble breathing" when a friend brought her to Abbotsford Regional Hospital in British Columbia on the night of January 30, 2017, according to the CBC. She was quickly seen by a doctor, who told the 56-year-old she was experiencing muscle spasms.[13] She was given a shot of morphine and sent home.

Murphy died two days later, on February 1.[14]

Her experience is unfortunately common in Canada, where overcrowding often leaves hospital staff unable to devote proper attention to emergency room patients.

The day Murphy died, Jack Webb was taking his final breaths in a hospital on the other side of the country. The 68-year-old had been diagnosed with pancreatic cancer on January 12, 2017. By that time, it had already spread to his liver and adrenal glands.[15]

Two weeks later, Webb was having trouble breathing and was admitted to the emergency department of Halifax's largest hospital. His wife later recalled to CTV that when he was finally seen by a doctor, they were told he was "the sickest man to arrive...that night."[16]

Yet Webb spent the next five days in agony as a result of hospital over-crowding. For the duration of his stay, Halifax Infirmary was under a "code census." According to CTV, this is "an overcrowding protocol that spills excess patients into the main hospital's hallways, sets off bed bumping and is a wider sign of a hospital beyond its capacity."[17]

As a result, over the next five days Webb was bumped from room to room, occasionally sharing space with several other patients. At one point, he spent six hours in a cold hallway. The night before he died, one hospital staffer callously yelled to another, "If he stops breathing, don't resuscitate!" Webb and his family were in earshot the whole time.[18]

His wife later learned that protocol dictated he should have been seen by a specialist immediately after he arrived.[19] The circumstances surrounding Webb's death prompted the Halifax Infirmary to rewrite its wait time rules.[20]

Single-payer systems make even children wait for care. In November

2017, three-year-old Basil Mohammed entered Birmingham Children's Hospital in the United Kingdom. The young boy suffered from Wolcott-Rallison syndrome, a rare disease that can cause liver or kidney failure, according to BBC News.[21]

He was seen by a triage nurse 15 minutes after he arrived but then waited over an hour for follow-up care, per the *Daily Mail*.[22] His father warned hospital staff that his son was going to die, to no avail.

Mohammed died in his father's arms, still waiting to be seen.[23]

Canadians aren't even in the clear when they make it into the clinic. Canadian doctors commonly prohibit patients from discussing more than one issue per appointment.[24] If patients have more to ask about, they are encouraged to make another appointment. For physicians, this may save time. But for patients, it could mean getting in line once again.

THE DOCTOR IS OUT

The Canadian health care system doesn't have the capacity to meet demand. In 2018, Canada had fewer than three doctors—and fewer than three beds—for every 1,000 residents.[25] In 2019, an estimated 175,000 people in Canada's four easternmost provinces were waiting to be matched with a family doctor.[26] If current trends continue, Canada will be short 60,000 full-time nurses by 2022, according to the Canadian Nurses Association.[27]

Canadian officials don't appear particularly interested in narrowing their doctor shortage. One in five newly certified medical and surgical specialists can't find a job in Canada, according to a May 2019 report from the Royal College of Physicians and Surgeons of Canada. Neurosurgeons, radiation oncologists, and orthopedic surgeons are most likely to be unemployed.[28]

That makes little sense, given that Canadians wait longer for orthopedic surgery than for any other specialty procedure.

Provincial governments don't appear to have the money to hire the doctors their residents need—or don't care to find it. "We have unemployed orthopedic surgeons who are dying to meet this need," said Mark Glazebrook, the head of the Canadian Orthopaedic Association. "The government can't afford it."[29]

And because private insurance is illegal under the Canada Health Act, Canadian patients don't have an escape route from single-payer health care. Some people are trying to change that.

FIGHTING FOR CARE

The *Chaoulli* decision legalized the sale of private insurance—but only in Quebec. A market for private insurance hasn't taken off in Quebec—and would be unlikely to launch in any other province that legalized private coverage—because Canadian doctors are generally prohibited from billing patients or private insurers directly if they also want to participate in the single-payer system.

Dr. Brian Day, an orthopedic surgeon and the former president of the Canadian Medical Association, has been fighting that prohibition for years. In 1996, he opened the Cambie Surgery Centre, a for-profit clinic in Vancouver, British Columbia.[30] He established the center because "we had doctors who had patients who needed surgery but there was no place for them to work."[31]

Cambie is one of a handful of private medical centers scattered throughout Canada. Private centers like Cambie originally came about to treat military personnel, Royal Canadian Mounted Police (RCMP), and other groups exempt from single-payer.

Over the years, these private clinics have proliferated. For example, there were 74 private diagnostic clinics operating in 2018—compared to just three MRI clinics in 1994.[32]

Day says clinics like his perform over 60,000 surgeries a year. Workers' Compensation Boards have been among his most enthusiastic supporters. They'd rather pay for quick care for disabled workers—and get them back on the job and off disability—than send them checks while they wait for care through the single-payer system.

Indeed, if private clinics didn't handle those tens of thousands of surgeries, the government would have to foot the bill. As a result, Day claims private clinics save the government hundreds of millions of dollars annually.[33]

"Code Gridlock in Canada"

Long waits for care are a fact of life for Canadian patients. In February 2018, Ontario native Leo Seguin went to the hospital after hurting his back. The hospital was crowded, so Seguin spent 10 days recovering in a hospital bathroom, which staffers jokingly called "the spa." He was baffled by the placement of the bed, which left his head next to the toilet, but was otherwise unperturbed.[34]

Seguin shared his story with the CBC. "I didn't hear nobody moaning…so when I slept at night, I slept like a log," he said.[35]

Not all patients are so lucky. On March 25, 2017, Jamie-Lee Ball arrived at Brampton Civic Hospital in Ontario in "excruciating pain." According to the CBC, she had undergone abdominal surgery the previous month and knew her condition might be serious. Soon after she arrived, a doctor determined she was bleeding internally and might need a blood transfusion.[36]

Yet Ball spent five days on a stretcher in the hallway, "screaming in pain and crying." The hospital had declared a "Code Gridlock," meaning it was at capacity and no longer able to put patients in beds. At one point, she was booted from her "prime" spot in the hallway to accommodate a cancer patient. She told the CBC that "everyone shared a single public bathroom."[37]

Ball's situation may seem enviable to Kelly Yerxa, who spent 47 hours waiting for surgery after falling down a flight of stairs. According to *Toronto Life*, "Bones were sticking out of [Yerxa's] right elbow, and her wrists were in the shape of the letter S." She also had multiple broken ribs and a lacerated kidney.[38]

She was placed in the "orange zone," a section of the hallway where hospital beds are stacked up like sardines. There was nowhere for her family to stand, and her bed was next to a bedpan dumping station.[39]

Looking back at her dismal experience, Yerxa is grateful for how much pain she was in. As *Toronto Life*'s reporting put it, "Had she been more lucid, she would have been angry."[40]

Day has spent the past decade in the throes of a lawsuit challenging the ban on clinics charging patients directly for care.[41] His trial finally ended in July 2019, after three years before British Columbia's Supreme Court.[42] His provincial government has done everything it can to delay, distract, and outspend him, in hopes he'll give up the fight.

The government claims it's upholding the principle of equity in health care. But what good is equity if it means everyone is waiting the same amount of time for necessary care? Equity can't heal someone with a serious illness—or pay someone's wages while they languish on a wait list, unable to work.

LOOKING FOR CARE ANYWHERE BUT HERE

Canadians who can't or won't wait for treatment have another option—go abroad.

SecondStreet.org obtained data from Canada's national statistics agency to determine how many Canadians left the country to obtain medical care. They found that in 2017, Canadian patients made between 217,500 and 323,700 trips abroad.[43] Ontario had the highest number of medical tourists—as many as 208,400 patients in 2017.[44]

The motives, costs, and destinations vary, but one thing is certain—an increasing number of Canadians want out of single-payer health care.

"Vacationing at Hospitals Abroad"

Many Brits and Canadians love traveling to warmer climes. Some head there not to relax on the beach but to seek medical care they can't get in their home countries.

Take Clare Mullarkey of Oldbury, West Midlands, in England. She was diagnosed with multiple sclerosis in 2011, when she was just 22. Six years later, Mullarkey's condition had worsened, to the point where it was impeding her work and daily life.[45]

In October 2017, her doctor recommended her for a hematopoietic stem-cell transplantation (HSCT)[46]—an intense chemotherapy that wipes out and regrows a patient's immune system.[47]

After eight months, the National Health Service denied Mullarkey's request for treatment. She was told she was "not ill enough" to receive HSCT, according to the *Mirror*. She didn't want to wait for another relapse, which she feared would leave her using a wheelchair.[48]

So she sought treatment in Mexico. As of March 2019, Mullarkey had completed the first stage of the procedure and had raised almost one-third of the £65,000 necessary for treatment.[49]

Angela Bugera, a 51-year-old art gallery owner from Edmonton, Alberta, waited six months to see a specialist about her hip pain. Bugera was already reduced to walking with a cane and felt that things were bound to get worse.[50]

After a five-minute appointment confirmed she was a candidate for a hip replacement, she discovered she'd have to wait even longer to have the procedure, according to CTV News.[51]

Like Mullarkey, Bugera took things into her own hands. In 2015, she paid over C$18,000 to have her hip replaced at Health City Cayman Islands. By June 2017, she was happy with her choice, Yahoo! News reported.[52]

Bugera remained a single-payer supporter but offered a frank assessment of the problems facing Canada's health care system. "Universal health care is very important, but our system is overwhelmed and we should be looking at options to supplement it until it can support us all again," she said.[53]

Perhaps a better solution is to more fully deploy the market principles at work in the private health care systems that have helped Mullarkey, Bugera, and so many others in their time of need.

IN HER MAJESTY'S NATIONAL HEALTH SERVICE

Just as in Canada, health care in the United Kingdom is defined by long waits, shortages of doctors and nurses, few resources, and unhappy patients.

As of May 2019, 4.34 million people were waiting for treatment throughout England, a 42 percent increase from 2014.[54]

One of those patients was Susannah Thraves, a journalist who needed surgery on a damaged kidney.[55] In an August 2019 piece for *The Guardian*, Thraves wrote, "I can cope with the physical pain. But I really struggle to deal with the distress and anxiety of being on what seems like a never-ending waiting list."[56]

The National Health Service acknowledges it will keep people waiting. The "maximum waiting time for non-urgent consultant-led treatments" is 18 weeks after an appointment is booked.[57] The goal is for 92 percent of patients to be on the wait list for less than 18 weeks.[58]

As of May 2019, the NHS hadn't hit that target in over three years. In fact, the agency fails to stay within most of its own guardrails. In 2019, the Liberal Democrat party alleged the NHS missed its own treatment time guarantees 200 times per day.[59] Despite having a "zero tolerance" policy for patients waiting more than 52 weeks for care, as of May 2019 more than 1,000 patients had been left waiting for over a year.[60]

Cancer treatment targets are among the most frequently missed. The NHS aims to treat 85 percent of cancer patients within 62 days of a referral from a general practitioner. As of June 2019, the NHS hadn't hit that target since 2013.[61] According to a report released that same month, only 38 percent of NHS trusts met the 62-day treatment standard.[62] In March 2019, one doctor told the *Independent* that "more than 127,000 people have waited too long for cancer treatment since the target was first missed five years ago."[63]

"The Difference Between Life and Death—18 Minutes"

Five-year-old Ellie-May Clark was wheezing so badly she was unable to walk from school to her home in southeast Wales.[64]

She had first been treated for asthma months shy of her second birthday, so her mother Shanice didn't panic.[65] She called the Grange Clinic in Newport, Wales, and requested a home visit, according to BBC News. Instead, the clinic offered her an emergency appointment and told her to arrive in 25 minutes.[66]

Shanice Clark had an eight-week-old baby, in addition to five-year-old Ellie-May, and no car. She called the hospital to say she might be late. She'd need a few minutes to arrange for care for her newborn and wait for the bus.[67]

Ms. Clark claims she and her daughter arrived at the clinic five minutes late, per the BBC. The receptionist on duty at the time said they were 18 minutes late.[68]

Regardless, when they reached the front desk, the Clarks were informed they would have to return the following day.[69] Dr. Joanne Rowe, the physician in charge of "child safeguarding," had a rule for late patients—arrive more than 10 minutes late, and the appointment is canceled.[70]

According to the *Telegraph*, Dr. Rowe explained the rule thus: "If you have 25 patients to see in a morning or afternoon and a lot of people are 15 minutes late or 20 minutes late you are never going to be able to manage your work."[71]

Ellie-May was confused. She asked her mother, "Why won't the doctor see me?"[72]

Shanice Clark didn't know, and she was frustrated. She had warned them she would be late. She was certain the usual course of steroids would have relieved her daughter's symptoms. Besides, Dr. Rowe had previously received a letter explaining that Ellie-May was "at risk of having another episode of severe/life threatening asthma," according to the *Telegraph*.[73]

The *Telegraph* also reported that Dr. Rowe did not prominently record the letter in Ellie-May's medical records.[74] Not that it would have made much difference. Dr. Rowe didn't even open Ellie-May's file before refusing to see her, according to BBC News.[75]

As she would later testify, Shanice Clark took her daughter home and put her to bed.[76] She checked on her daughter every 10 minutes. Around 10:30

p.m., she heard Ellie-May coughing. She rushed into Ellie-May's room just as her daughter fell out of bed, her hands and face blue.[77]

Ellie-May was rushed to the hospital but died shortly thereafter.

After a lengthy inquest, a coroner determined that "Ellie-May Clark died of natural causes where the opportunity to provide potentially life-saving treatment was missed. The medical cause of death being . . . Bronchial asthma."[78]

The coroner concluded that the five-year-old was "let down by the failures in the system."[79]

A June 2019 British Medical Association investigation found that NHS hospitals frequently relied on "escalation beds," temporary beds that are usually reserved for emergencies, like a flu outbreak.[80] According to BMA consultants committee chair Dr. Rob Harwood, "The use of escalation beds is a sign that trusts are at a critical stage and are unable to cope with demand."[81]

Overcrowding of this nature makes it hard to process patients. Consider the NHS's four-hour wait target for Accident and Emergency departments.[82] Daily A&E use has increased every year since 2012, and the NHS can't keep up.[83] In 2018, close to 19 percent of people waited more than four hours in A&E departments.[84] Over 57,000 people waited more than four hours for admission in July 2019 alone. More than 400 patients waited longer than 12 hours.[85]

But nothing compares to January 2019. That month, A&E waits were the worst they'd been in 15 years, with close to 330,000 patients waiting longer than they should have.[86] That month, the NHS proposed scrapping the four-hour wait target altogether.[87]

WINTER IS COMING

A&E visits spike when flu season is in full swing. Poor responses from the NHS are so common that "winter crisis" has become a catchphrase in the British media.[88] Even against such a low bar, the 2017–2018 winter was particularly bad.

Nearly 23 percent of patients waited more than four hours to be admitted to Accident and Emergency departments, up from just over 6 percent in winter 2010–2011.[89] Once they were admitted, more than 221,000 people waited more than four hours to receive treatment.[90] They were the lucky ones.

During winter crises, patients in England can spend hours in ambulances before setting foot in a hospital. The number of beds available throughout the NHS has decreased while A&E visits have increased.[91] Ambulances often line up outside overcrowded hospitals, waiting for a space to open up for the patient they're carrying.[92]

The NHS's goal is for patients to be transferred from an ambulance to an A&E department within 15 minutes.[93] During the 2017–2018 winter crisis, over 180,000 of these so-called "handovers" took more than a half-hour. Some 42,000 took over an hour.[94]

Between Christmas and New Year's, nearly 17,000 people waited in the back of an ambulance—nearly 5,000 of them for more than an hour, according to *The Guardian*.[95]

Of course, this is all contingent upon getting an ambulance. From 2017 to 2018, ambulances routinely took more than 24 hours to respond to patient calls. One Welsh patient waited over 62 hours for an ambulance in 2017, according to BBC News.[96] Hospitals claimed these cases were "less serious" and patients had to wait while ambulances attended to patients with more life-threatening conditions.[97]

Ambulance operators are seriously short-staffed. More than 33,000 ambulance workers quit the NHS between 2010 and 2018.[98] The *Mirror* found that the NHS spent over £235 million on private ambulances to offset a paramedic shortage between 2015 and 2018. That's around £215,000 a day.[99] The paramedic shortage is so bad in parts of England that ambulance providers have proposed recruiting volunteers or enlisting military personnel as drivers.[100]

THE DOCTOR IS OUT, PART TWO

The paramedic shortage is just the tip of the iceberg. The NHS is plagued by shortages of other key personnel.

The reason is simple—people hate working for the NHS. It's easy to see why. Each week, close to 60 percent of its employees work unpaid overtime. Thanks to the stress, 40 percent of NHS employees report feeling "unwell." Around half want to leave their roles.[101]

According to the *Mirror*, each year more than one in four nurses take sick days due to stress.[102] More than 160,000 nurses have quit the NHS since 2011.[103]

Things aren't much better for doctors. One physician told *The Guardian* that working for the NHS has drained him of his humanity, since his workload made it impossible to have personal interactions with patients.[104]

British physicians aren't paid particularly well for their troubles, either. The average generalist physician in the United Kingdom makes US$134,671 a year. His counterpart in the United States takes in close to US$220,000 a year. General practitioners in Germany and Canada are also better paid than their peers in the United Kingdom.[105]

This combination of high-stress work and comparatively low pay has made it hard for the NHS to retain people. In 2018, the United Kingdom had just under three doctors and about eight nurses for every 1,000 patients.[106] That's the worst doctor-patient ratio of all EU countries.[107] As of December 2018, the NHS had over 9,000 doctor vacancies and over 39,000 nurse vacancies in England alone.[108] Toss in other staff, and total NHS vacancies rise to just under 95,000.[109]

Things are expected to get worse. About 9,000 doctors quit in 2017, according to *BMJ*.[110] A 2019 poll found that 42 percent of general practitioners were planning to quit by 2024.[111]

In March 2019, three of the United Kingdom's biggest think

tanks released a study examining the future of the health care workforce.[112] By 2029, there will be a shortage of "108,000 full-time equivalent nurses."[113] The NHS will be short 7,000 general practitioners by 2024, if current trends continue.[114]

To help combat the doctor shortage, in 2015 the NHS resolved to recruit 2,000 foreign general practitioners by 2020. As of June 2019, they only had 120.[115]

Experts from the King's Fund, a British think tank, have suggested that heads of hospitals fly to low-income countries to personally recruit nurses for their staffs.[116] In May 2019, the *Times* reported the NHS was planning to do just that. The organization hoped to recruit 5,000 foreign nurses each year until 2024.[117] Less than a month later, the NHS had reportedly scrapped the plan.[118]

Some of the NHS's actions seem to indicate they're not even trying to address the shortage of personnel. In January 2019, the NHS announced plans to recruit 22,000 "non-medical" staff to help divert patients away from general practitioners. That includes nurses and pharmacists as well as "social prescribers," who refer patients to "non-medical interventions like singing groups."[119]

TOO MANY PATIENTS, NOT ENOUGH SPACE

These massive staffing shortages cause more problems than wait times. Nine million patients had hospital appointments canceled in 2017–2018, up from just over 3 million a decade earlier.[120] In 2018, close to 80,000 elective operations were canceled the day the patient was supposed to have them.[121] Around 10 percent of those patients had not received treatment within 28 days of the cancellation.[122]

Additionally, close to 4,000 urgent operations were canceled at the last minute—150 of those were canceled for the second time or more.[123]

As the NHS continues to underperform, private health care has grown increasingly popular. The number of people with private coverage grew more than 2 percent in 2015.[124] That year, just over 10 percent of the population had private coverage—almost 4 million policies total.[125]

To help clear the surgery backlog, in March 2019 the NHS proposed paying for patients who had been on the waitlist for over 26 weeks to receive private care. That's about 250,000 patients.[126] Ironically, one study found that the NHS would be able to perform 300,000 more surgeries a year if hospitals simply organized schedules better.[127]

Meanwhile, cost-cutting is making it increasingly hard for patients to access care. A 2019 proposal to close one-third of specialist treatment centers could force stroke patients to travel 45 minutes for treatment.[128] Similar budget cuts have driven up wait times for cataract removals, one study found.[129]

"DIY Dentistry"

David Woodhouse, a 62-year-old resident of Cornwall, England, was experiencing tooth pain in the summer of 2017. He began looking for a dentist who would see him. After 18 months of searching, he still hadn't found one.[130]

An NHS emergency clinic offered to remove the tooth he claimed was causing him pain in December 2018. But David hesitated. Removing the tooth might have only fixed part of his problem. He had been having long-term issues with a dental plate.[131]

Eventually, he took matters into his own hands. "I got the needle-nose pliers and out it came," he told BBC News. "The removal itself was considerably less painful than the long-term pain I was experiencing."[132]

David is not the only one of his neighbors to struggle to find a dentist. According to the NHS, in January 2019, over 48,000 people in Devon and Cornwall were on waiting lists to see one. Only one dentist in Cornwall was accepting new patients.[133]

Patients in one town in Cornwall were a 65-mile round trip away from that dentist, according to the British Dental Association. To get there by public transit would have taken over three hours. Patients in Plymouth and South Wales faced similarly arduous journeys to their closest dentist.[134]

Things are only going to get worse. More than half of British dentists plan to retire or scale back their services by 2024.[135]

Do-it-yourself dentistry may soon be Britons' best option.

CHECKUPS: NOW A TEAM SPORT!

According to *BMJ*, the average appointment with a general practitioner in the United Kingdom lasts just over nine minutes. Appointment length has been increasing by 4.2 seconds per year, meaning the NHS is on track to meet the British Medical Association's recommended 15-minute appointment sometime in 2086.[136]

Some health officials believe that group appointments are a viable "solution" to this problem. Under this model, one general practitioner sees up to 15 patients with the same condition for around 90 minutes.[137] The NHS claims that group appointments can improve a patient's experience by giving them more time with a doctor and allowing them to meet other people with their condition.

During group appointments, patients may only spend two minutes with the actual doctor. The rest of the time is spent with a "facilitator," who could be anyone, including a "receptionist, clerk, or healthcare assistant with a day's training."[138]

Doctors have embraced group appointments for a variety of conditions, ranging from diabetes and arthritis to obesity and erectile dysfunction.[139]

Unfortunately, government-run health care deprives patients of more than just convenience. Patients in single-payer systems often have trouble accessing cutting-edge treatments and technologies— even when it's a matter of life and death.

CHAPTER FIVE

THE HORRORS OF SINGLE-PAYER INSURANCE—ACCESS TO CUTTING-EDGE TREATMENTS AND TECHNOLOGIES

C anada and the United Kingdom lag far behind the United States in providing patients access to the latest treatments—including prescription drugs, diagnostic tests, and cutting-edge medical technology and equipment like computed tomography (CT) scanners and magnetic resonance imaging (MRI) machines.

The chronic shortage of treatments and technologies is a result of the rationing schemes and price controls that government-run, single-payer systems inevitably utilize to rein in costs. No one says no to a free diagnostic test or a free treatment. So health authorities in Canada and Britain say no for them.

A WAITING GAME FOR CUTTING-EDGE TECHNOLOGY IN CANADA

Take CT scanners—medical imaging devices used to detect and diagnose a number of conditions, including cancer.[1] In 2017, Canada had less than 16 machines for every million people, according to the Organisation for Economic Co-operation and Development (OECD). The United States had 42 per million people—2.6 times as many.[2]

Less than 15 percent of rural emergency departments, which serve 20 percent of Canadians, had a CT scanner in 2017.[3] Each of the country's three northern territories had just one scanner—in total.[4] It's no wonder the average wait for a CT scan across the country is more than four weeks, according to the Fraser Institute.[5] Even when Canadians get CT scans, there's almost a one in four chance that the machine being used is over 10 years old.[6]

Canada's 13 provincial and territorial governments choose which hospitals get scanners and which don't. Despite the combination of tax revenue and federal funding they receive, they can't seem to provide scanners to every hospital.

As a result, some hospitals have to fend for themselves. It took 10 years for one hospital in Sudbury, Ontario, to raise enough money to buy one. A nearby hospital in Windsor had its machine replaced after less than a year's wait.[7]

MRI machines are just as hard to come by in Canada. There are 366 of them spread throughout the country.[8] That equates to less than 10 units per million people. The United States has close to 40 MRI units per million people.[9]

Consequently, wait times for MRIs in Canada average over 10 weeks, according to Fraser.[10] More than one in four MRI machines in Canada are at least a decade old.[11]

According to a study by the Conference Board of Canada, close to 400,000 people are forced to exit the workforce each year as they wait for CT and MRI scans. All told, these "excessive wait times" cost the economy $3.54 billion in 2017.[12]

The story is the same for radiotherapy machines, like X-rays. The United States has four times as many per million people as does Canada, according to OECD figures.[13]

Then there's the discrepancy in mammography machines, which are used to detect breast cancer. Canada has 18 of them per million people; the United States has just under 60 per million.[14]

"SORRY, THAT DRUG IS UNAVAILABLE, EH?"

The public sector covers less than half of drug spending in Canada.[15] But the government still exercises outsized control over the country's drug market.

Many of the most cutting-edge drugs are in short supply in Canada, if they're available at all. One analysis of 290 new medicines brought to market between 2011 and 2018 showed that less than half were available in Canada. U.S. patients had access to 89 percent of those new drugs.[16]

The numbers are even more dire in specific categories of treatment. Of 21 new treatments for blood disorders introduced between 2011 and 2018, Canadian patients have access to just 14 percent. All 21 were available in the United States.[17]

Canadians have access to less than half as many new central nervous system therapies as Americans. Only 59 percent of the 82 new cancer drugs are available in Canada, whereas 96 percent of them were accessible to American patients.[18]

Canadians can blame the price controls their government has levied on medicines for their inability to access them. The country's Patented Medicine Prices Review Board sets a maximum price for each new drug before approving it for sale.[19] Drug manufacturers may respond by refusing to sell their products in Canada at all—or by making only small quantities available.

Consequently, scarcity plagues the Canadian drug market. In 2018, there was a mass shortage of EpiPens—and in 2017, a shortage of the common antidepressant Wellbutrin.[20]

According to a CBC report, Canada experienced 25 drug shortages in a one-week period in September 2018. Critical medications for Parkinson's disease, schizophrenia, and hepatitis B suddenly became unavailable.[21] There's even a government-chartered website listing all the drugs Canada is short on.[22]

Drug shortages are so rampant that one in four Canadians has been personally affected by them or knows someone who has, according to a survey from the Canadian Pharmacists Association.[23]

Even if drug manufacturers assent to the Canadian government's price controls, they still have to compete to get onto the formularies of provincial health plans. The Common Drug Review process is conducted by the Canadian Agencies for Drugs and Technology in Health (CADTH), which considers the clinical and cost-effectiveness of a drug.[24] Then, the Canadian Drug Expert Committee makes a reimbursement recommendation. Each provincial health plan decides, based on the committee's recommendation, whether to put a drug on its formulary.[25]

These may sound like reasonable consumer protections—a way to ensure that people get the best prices possible. But what if you need a drug that doesn't make it onto the formulary? You're generally out of luck.

That's a particular problem for people with rare diseases. Canada is one of the only developed countries not to have a policy for the development and availability of so-called orphan drugs. Such drugs are expensive to develop, in part because there's a small market of potential customers for them.[26]

Only a few provinces have funds set up to cover orphan drugs. Even when they are covered, very few are available, and not for all rare diseases.[27]

Consider the plight of eight-year-old Andre Larocque and his six-year-old brother, Joshua, who both have cystic fibrosis. Their family lives in Ontario, which doesn't cover the drugs the boys need to adequately treat the disease. In a last-ditch effort to treat their sons, Sasha Haughian and Jamie Larocque enrolled their boys in a trial for a new drug called Symedko.[28]

Andre was chosen, but Joshua wasn't—meaning he had to go without treatment. Sasha described this unimaginable situation to CBC. "When I put them to bed at night, I hear Andre go to sleep peacefully and then I hear Josh laying awake in his bed coughing himself to sleep," she said.[29]

Some Canadians have to engage in medical tourism within their own country for other crucial treatments, including organ transplants. According to a 2019 report conducted by the CBC, lung transplants "cannot be done in Atlantic Canada"—the provinces of New Brunswick, Newfoundland, Nova Scotia, and Prince Edward Island. So patients have to travel hundreds of miles away to the likes of Toronto to undergo the procedure. Their living expenses, much of which they have to cover out of pocket, can run in the tens of thousands of dollars. Some have lost their homes trying to cover them.[30]

"Canadian Cancer Refugee"

Sharon Shemblaw was the kind of person who always carried around fruit and two-dollar coins—"toonies," as they're called—to give the homeless. So beloved by her community was the dedicated volunteer that her children's school once shut down to throw her a birthday party.[31]

The 46-year-old mother of three was in excellent health when she was diagnosed with acute myeloid leukemia (AML) in August 2015, according to a report published by the *Toronto Star* in May 2016.[32] Doctors told Shemblaw she was a "prime candidate" for an allogeneic stem-cell transplant, which replaces a patient's cancerous bone marrow with healthy blood cells from a donor.[33]

AML patients who receive a transplant while in remission have a 20 to 25 percent chance of surviving.[34] Shemblaw was told she had an 80 percent chance.[35]

There was just one problem. Her local hospital, Princess Margaret Cancer Centre in Ontario, didn't have the resources to treat her. Doctors recommend AML patients receive a stem-cell transplant "no longer than two to three months" after their cancer has gone into remission.[36]

In 2016, the year Shemblaw sought treatment, the average wait at Princess Margaret was six to eight months, according to the *Star*.[37]

The Ontario Ministry of Health agreed to spend $100 million sending cancer patients to the United States for stem-cell transplants. Hospitals in Buffalo, Detroit, and Cleveland agreed to accept over 200 sick Ontarians.[38]

Patients who wished to receive treatment in the United States needed to commit to three months away from home and bring a full-time caretaker.[39] That wouldn't be cheap, of course. So most patients opted not to go.

Shemblaw was one of the few who made the journey.[40] Finally in remission after three rounds of chemotherapy, she headed to the Roswell Park Cancer Institute in Buffalo with her daughter, who had taken time off from her doctoral program to be her mother's caretaker.[41]

By the time Shemblaw arrived in Buffalo, the cancer had returned.[42] At the time, a Health Ministry policy refused to cover stem-cell transplants for patients who weren't in remission, even though the procedure would likely be just as effective in treating the disease.

That policy has since been overturned.[43]

Denied treatment, Shemblaw returned to Ontario, where she underwent experimental chemotherapy. The procedure was ineffective and yielded a bladder infection so painful that she hallucinated for nearly two weeks.[44]

On May 4, 2016, Shemblaw's husband brought his wife a bouquet of her favorite pink tulips. Looking at him with eyes wide open, she began repeating, "I want to see them, I want to see them." She had gone blind.[45]

She died the next day.

The Canadian government also limits access to treatment by arbitrarily defining some treatments as "medically necessary" and some not.

The Canada Health Act grants the government a monopoly on covering anything deemed medically necessary but never defines that phrase. Each province has its own take on what's medically necessary.[46] Some common procedures that have ended up on the chopping block include wart removals and varicose vein treatments.[47]

Over the years, Canadian lawmakers have attempted to add prescription drug coverage to the country's national health plan. In 2004, Prime Minister Paul Martin unsuccessfully pushed for a "Pharmacare" plan, saying "there's something profoundly Canadian about this idea."[48]

In 2019, the Liberal government led by Prime Minister Justin Trudeau introduced its own Pharmacare program.[49] The proposal would create a new federal agency, which would determine which drugs were cost-effective. The aim of this program is not to increase access but to standardize drug coverage across all provinces and territories.[50] Just as in the rest of the country's single-payer system, Pharmacare would put equity over access—at the expense of Canadian patients.

It's hard to consider Canada's health care system "universal" if so many of the treatments and technologies at the heart of modern medicine are unavailable.

BRITAIN'S LOW-TECH HEALTH CARE SYSTEM

The United Kingdom's National Health Service is even more technologically retrograde than Canada's.

The OECD's most recent data on CT scanners in Great Britain come from 2014. In that year, there were a little over nine for every million Britons. That's less than one-fourth the number available to American patients that year.[51]

Mammography machines are also sparse in the British Isles. In 2011, the most recent year for which the OECD has data, there were just over 10 mammography machines for every million British residents. That year, there were almost 40 per million people in the United States; today, it's 60 per million.[52]

Want an MRI in Britain? Good luck. The United Kingdom had just seven MRI machines per million residents in 2014—less than one-fifth as many as the United States.[53]

This is all bad news for those at risk of cancer or heart disease. In 2017, the Royal College of Radiologists estimated that over 56,000 patients with angina, a type of chest pain, were unable to access a CT scanner due to shortages. A sufficient number of the machines could have prevented thousands of heart attacks a year by empowering doctors to potentially catch patients' heart problems before they became acute.[54]

"Accept Our Shoddy Care—or We'll Throw You in Jail"

Each year in the United Kingdom, just under 90 children will be diagnosed with a rare form of brain cancer called medulloblastoma.[55] In 2014, six-year-old Ashya King was one of them.

Medulloblastoma originates in the cerebellum, the part of the brain near the base of the skull that controls balance and other complex motor and cognitive functions.[56] The cancer can spread throughout the rest of the brain and to the spinal cord.[57]

Ashya was first diagnosed in the summer of 2014. He had his tumor removed on July 24 that year, according to BBC News. After a second surgery on August 22, the NHS recommended radiotherapy to round out his treatment.[58]

His parents pushed back. According to the *Telegraph*, Brett and Naghmeh King were nervous that their son was too weak to withstand traditional radiation therapy.[59] The *Daily Mail* reports that they requested Ashya receive proton therapy instead.[60]

X-rays—the heart of radiation therapy—can cause damage to healthy cells they come into contact with. So they could harm vital organs near tumors, especially if those organs are still developing, as they are in children. Proton therapy is far more targeted, and thus poses a lower risk of inflicting collateral damage on other parts of the body.[61]

In the United States, cancer patients have had access to proton therapy since 2001.[62] Construction on the first proton therapy center in the United Kingdom began 16 years later, in 2017.[63]

Doctors at Southampton General Hospital would not recommend proton therapy for Ashya, the BBC News reported.[64] This put his parents in a bind. Naghmeh King later told the *Telegraph*, "If we had left Ashya with the NHS in Britain, he would not be with us today."[65]

So on August 28, 2014, the Kings took their son to Spain to seek alternative treatment.[66] Hospital staff reported the boy missing, and an international arrest warrant on suspicion of neglect was issued for the Kings.[67] Two days later, Ashya's parents were arrested and thrown in a Madrid jail.[68] For 72 hours, Ashya was "placed under armed guard in a Spanish hospital, where he howled with despair and confusion," according to the *Daily Mail*.[69]

Facing an international outcry, a British court granted the Kings permission to take their son to the Proton Therapy Center in Prague on September 5.[70] At the time, the *Telegraph* reported that doctors there had "every reason to hope [Ashya would] make a full recovery."[71]

In March 2018, three years after he began treatment, the *Telegraph* reported that Ashya King was cancer free.[72]

In 2018, the NHS recommended an advanced type of MRI for men at risk for prostate cancer. But the Royal College of Radiologists said there weren't enough MRI machines to cover the number of scans needed. The machines that were available were too old.[73]

The Royal College told the *Independent* that 90 percent of MRI machines in Britain were over 5 years old; 30 percent were over 10 years old.[74]

British patients must make do with outdated technology, if they can gain access to it at all, because the National Health Service is perpetually short on money. A 2018 study by Birmingham University and the Health Foundation found that budget cuts were the primary reason the country's technology was outdated.[75]

Another Health Foundation study found that the United Kingdom's health care capital spending as a share of GDP was 0.2 percentage points lower than the OECD average. Meeting that average would take another £3 billion per year.[76]

BRITAIN'S NOT-SO-NICE WAY TO RATION DRUGS

The United Kingdom has made the rationing of innovative medicines an art form.

The NHS is effectively the sole buyer of prescription drugs in the country. As a monopsonist, it can and does dictate the price of medicine in the United Kingdom.

Since 1957, British pharmaceutical companies have "voluntarily" signed on to the Pharmaceutical Price Regulation Scheme

(PPRS). Under this scheme, the profits from branded drugs are restricted to keep prices low.[77] If a manufacturer refuses to accept the price the NHS sets, then its wares are unavailable to British patients.

Manufacturers that aren't part of the PPRS are subject to still more direct price controls. The Branded Health Service Medicines Prices Regulations subject each new drug brought to market to a maximum price.[78] Some manufacturers simply opt not to sell their products in Britain rather than accept a lowball offer from the NHS.

Of the 243 medicines across 15 therapeutic categories launched worldwide between 2011 and 2018, just two-thirds were available in the United Kingdom. That's slightly more than were available in Canada. But it's far less than the 88 percent on offer in the United States.[79]

In some categories, the discrepancy between the United Kingdom and its former colony is even more startling. For example, only 36 percent of new dermatology treatments that hit the market between 2011 and 2018 were available in Britain. Eighty-two percent were available in the United States.[80]

Fifty-three percent of new diabetes medications made their way to the United Kingdom, compared to 67 percent in the United States. Fifty-seven of 74 new cancer drugs launched in the United Kingdom during that time period; 70 of those 74 did so in the United States.[81]

The NHS relies on the work of NICE to determine the "proper" price for drugs and other treatments. NICE's primary metric for calculating whether a treatment is worth its price tag is the Quality-Adjusted Life Year, or QALY.

The metric effectively puts a dollar—or rather, a pound—sign on a patient's life.

The QALY of a treatment is calculated by multiplying how much longer that treatment will extend a person's life by the quality of life the patient will have.[82] If a treatment will cause a person to live

10 more years but with a quality of life half that of a fully healthy person, the treatment would have a QALY value of five.

Those quality-of-life measurements aren't exactly scientific. Patients who take part in clinical trials for new treatments take surveys that grade their health across five dimensions. Those five grades are then distilled into one number between zero and one, where one is perfect health and zero is death.[83] That number is the quality-of-life score.

The QALY values for new treatments are then compared with current options. Take our hypothetical new one, with its QALY value of five. Suppose that the current frontline therapy offers a QALY value of three. The new treatment thus offers a net gain of two QALYs.

NICE then determines whether those additional QALYs are worth the cost of the new treatment.[84] If a new therapy with a net gain of two QALYs costs £100,000 more than the old treatment, that's £50,000 per QALY gained.[85]

In NICE's book, £50,000 is way too much to spend for an additional year of life. The agency holds that only new treatments that cost less than £20,000 per QALY are worth paying for. Those between £20,000 and £30,000 per QALY are subject to stricter scrutiny of their supposed cost-effectiveness. Those beyond £30,000 per QALY have little hope of getting NICE's approval, except in rare circumstances.[86]

In other words, NICE has determined that it's generally not worth paying more than £20,000—a little over $25,000—for a drug or treatment that can give someone an additional year of life.

If the NHS follows NICE's guidelines and declines to cover the treatment, tough luck. Perhaps you'd be willing to travel abroad, to pay for the treatment on your own in another country where it's available?

These aren't hypotheticals. The NHS routinely denies patients access to treatments deemed too expensive or insufficiently cost-effective.

"Sorry, That Lifesaving Drug Is Too Expensive"

Christina Walker and her husband had never heard of cystic fibrosis before their son, Luis, was diagnosed with the genetic disorder at just three weeks old.[87] CF causes serious lung infections that hamper breathing—and can lead to liver damage and infertility. People with the disorder only live into their mid- to late 30s, on average.[88]

Luis's weakened immune system struggles to fight off even common colds, which routinely land him in the hospital. Since cystic fibrosis hinders digestion, a stomach bug can leave Luis emaciated, even if he eats constantly.[89]

In a column for *The Guardian*, Ms. Walker described her son's three-hour treatment regimen: "Every day he takes 22 tablets, three nebulisers, two inhalers, nasal sprays and lots of supplements."[90]

Fortunately, there's hope for Luis Walker and the over 70,000 people worldwide living with cystic fibrosis.[91] In 2015, the FDA approved Orkambi, a drug that can slow CF's impact on the lungs.[92]

But there's been a problem. Until late 2019, the drug wasn't available to British patients because the government believed Orkambi wasn't worth its price. In October of that year, the NHS and Vertex Pharmaceuticals, the drug's maker, finally reached a deal to supply the treatment to British patients.[93]

Boston-based Vertex initially offered Orkambi to the NHS for £105,000 per patient.[94] That's around $136,000—considerably less than the $272,000 Orkambi goes for in the United States.[95]

Perhaps it shouldn't be surprising that the NHS balked at covering a breakthrough drug. Testifying before the House of Commons in early 2019, NHS medical director Stephen Powis seemed appalled that "Vertex has come at this with a particular price in mind," rather than capitulating to the government's demands.[96]

The NHS's four-year refusal to pay for the drug has been bad news for patients. One of every ten people with cystic fibrosis worldwide lives in England.[97] Over 3,000 people in England, Scotland, Ireland, and Wales would benefit from Orkambi, according to the Cystic Fibrosis Trust, a patient advocacy group.[98]

Before striking its agreement with Vertex, the government threatened to invoke "crown use," a provision that allows the government to invalidate a drug's patent and manufacture a cheap generic.[99]

That may help the current crop of patients. But it would deprive pharmaceutical companies of revenue they could use to develop cures for tomorrow's patients. It would also discourage investors from funding expensive, risky drug research. Why bother plowing money into drug companies if the government will simply seize the fruits of their research? Investors will seek returns for their money in other sectors.

Invalidating patents is akin to declaring that we're fine with the current state of medical innovation—no more cures are necessary. Patients with the likes of cancer or cystic fibrosis, who are anxious for a miracle, would certainly beg to differ.

In June 2018, NHS England announced it would no longer routinely cover 17 "unnecessary" procedures—including injections for back pain, tonsil removal, breast reduction, and removal of bone spurs for shoulder pain—just so it could save £200 million a year. Per reporting from *The Guardian*, government officials tell patients "they have a responsibility to the NHS not to request useless treatment."[100]

NICE issued guidance in 2018 that recommended the NHS refuse to make abiraterone, a new treatment for prostate cancer that could give a patient 15 more months to live, the standard course of therapy. The rationing body instead urged health officials to require men suffering from prostate cancer to go through the status quo regimen of chemotherapy and hormones first.[101]

Prostate Cancer UK, a patient advocacy group, told the *Telegraph* that patients with late-stage cancer need the new drug as a primary treatment because they can't tolerate chemotherapy.[102]

NICE isn't Britain's only rationing body. In many cases, regional clinical commissioning groups (CCGs) determine whether a treatment will be covered by the NHS in their jurisdiction.[103] In recent years, those groups have become relentless, rationing even the most routine operations and commonly prescribed medications.

Take cataract removal. In March 2019, 104 of 195 CCGs would not cover this operation because they deemed it "a procedure of limited clinical value," according to data from the Medical Technology Group, a watchdog.[104] Seventy-six CCGs wouldn't let patients undergo cataract removal until they'd reached a certain level of sight loss. That "test" directly contradicts NICE guidelines.[105]

As of June 2019, patients in Herefordshire waited over five months on average for cataract operations.[106] One patient in Leeds fell while waiting close to 18 weeks for a surgery and injured his hip in the process.[107]

Other common procedures and treatments that have come under attack from CCGs due to their "limited clinical value" include hernia removal, continuous glucose monitoring, and hip and knee replacements.[108]

It's hard to believe that procedures that can prevent blindness or allow people to walk are "of limited clinical value."

"Missed Appointment? Sorry, No Treatment for You"

Bonnie Frost was given just eight months to live after the NHS denied her a lifesaving liver transplant in February 2018, according to Wales Online.[109]

The 50-year-old native of Barry, Wales, suffered from a rare autoimmune disorder called primary biliary cholangitis.[110] The disorder causes the immune system to mistakenly attack the bile ducts in the liver, which are necessary for digestion and help the body discard toxins, cholesterol, and deteriorated red blood cells.[111]

Like all autoimmune disorders, primary biliary cholangitis leaves the body vulnerable to other diseases. Jaundice and osteoporosis are common, as are memory loss and other mental impairments. Ultimately, the disease can result in liver scarring and failure and even liver cancer.[112]

Frost was first diagnosed in 2007 and placed on the transplant list by the liver specialist at Queen Elizabeth Hospital in Birmingham, England.[113] Five months later, she received a liver transplant. She was healthy until 2012, when her body began to reject the organ.[114]

Doctors told her she would only survive if she received a second liver transplant. But after being assessed for suitability at both Queen Elizabeth Hospital and King's College Hospital in London, Frost was denied a second transplant.[115]

Patients are generally denied liver transplants when doctors determine that the procedure would be ineffective or when the patient in question is an alcoholic or drug addict. None of these was the case for Frost. Doctors did not have a medical reason for denying her a transplant, according to reporting conducted by the *Mirror*.[116]

Why wouldn't the NHS approve a transplant for Bonnie Frost? The *Mirror* said it was because she had missed medical appointments six years earlier, when her body first began rejecting the liver.[117]

A single mother of three, Frost was working at the time as a special education teaching assistant. She struggled to make the eight-hour round trip to the hospital in Birmingham, 120 miles away from her home.[118] These trips became even more onerous as her health deteriorated. On top of that, hospital officials routinely rescheduled her appointments at the last minute.[119]

After being denied a new liver, Frost had to receive blood transfusions every six weeks just to stay alive.[120] When her hemoglobin levels drop between transfusions, she struggles to get by. She told Wales Online, "I'm basically helpless because I go dizzy if I stand so my balance is off. I get breathless trying to do anything so pretty much have to rely on others for everything."[121]

Frost and her family are frustrated with the NHS's refusal to treat her. "I just don't understand how if I haven't done anything really bad they can just let me die," she said. "It just makes me so angry."[122]

Her mother, Irene O'Brien, perfectly summed up the bureaucratic nightmare of the NHS's decision. "It's a stupid situation...she's my daughter. Who has the right to tell me I cannot have my daughter?"[123]

When CCGs won't cover these operations, doctors can submit individual funding requests to lobby the groups to make an exception. A study from *BMJ* found that there were nearly 74,000 such funding requests nationwide in 2016–2017. That was an increase of 20 percent from 2015–2016—and 47 percent higher than 2013–2014.[124]

CCGs have also limited what medications doctors can prescribe. A 2017 survey of specialists found that 7 in 10 doctors said they couldn't prescribe approved medications due to financial constraints from their local CCG.[125]

Whether it's through price controls, rationing, litmus tests, NICE guidance, or CCGs, the NHS seems determined to give patients in the United Kingdom as little access as possible to the best and newest treatments—all in the name of saving the government a few quid. Americans can expect similar outcomes if we adopt a single-payer system.

CHAPTER SIX

THE HORRORS OF SINGLE-PAYER INSURANCE—FINANCIAL COSTS

H umorist P.J. O'Rourke famously quipped, "If you think health
care is expensive now, wait until you see what it costs when
it's free."[1] Canada and the United Kingdom reveal exactly
how much "free" health care costs.

The two countries appear to spend less than the United States on
health care. U.S. health expenditures are notoriously high—about
17 percent of GDP. Canada's tab, by contrast, is a bit over 10 percent
of GDP; the United Kingdom's, a bit under 10 percent.[2]

But Canadians and the British pay far more than those numbers
may suggest. As we've seen, they must deal with substantial indi-
rect and non-monetary costs: lack of access to care, shortages and
chronic delays, and increased levels of pain and suffering.

What's more, the direct costs of single-payer care are greater
than its advocates claim. Canadians and Britons face monumental
taxes—and still must pay for a significant share of their care out
of pocket. Both countries are facing health cost crises that will
require massive amounts of new public spending or even more
draconian rationing schemes to solve.

SPIRALING COSTS

Neither Canada nor the United Kingdom has been able to keep its health costs under control. From 2005 to 2018, inflation-adjusted national health spending in the United Kingdom climbed 58 percent, according to data from the OECD. In Canada, it increased 50 percent.

In the United States, by contrast, national health spending grew 44 percent—a lower rate than either single-payer paradise.[3]

In Britain, health spending grew from 6 percent of GDP to just under 10 percent of GDP between 2000 and 2018.[4] To keep the system from imploding, the British government is pumping more money into the NHS. In June 2018, the then prime minister Theresa May announced that the NHS would get a £20.5 billion spending boost over the next five years as a 70th "birthday present."[5] This funding boost comes on top of a £1.8 billion increase it got in 2017.[6]

Critics have denounced May's plan as insufficient to deal with the NHS's current money problems, much less improve its quality of care. The Institute for Public Policy Research, a London-based think tank, called the funding boost "generous" but said, "It will not fund significant improvements in care unless the NHS radically increases productivity."[7]

Canada's attempts to control costs haven't been working either. Between 2001 and 2016, health spending by Canada's provinces shot up 116.4 percent. Health bills now consume anywhere from 34 percent to 43 percent of provincial budgets.[8]

As in the United Kingdom, health spending has been growing much faster than Canada's overall economy. In 2000, health care accounted for just over 8 percent of Canadian GDP. By 2015, it was more than 10 percent of GDP.[9] And in 2018, the Canadian Institute for Health Information pegged health spending at 11.3 percent of GDP—more than C$6,800 per capita.[10]

The upward march of health spending in both countries is likely to continue as their populations age.

GROWING TAX BURDEN

One of the problems with single-payer systems is that nobody knows exactly how much their care costs.

In Canada and the United Kingdom, health costs are covered mostly by general tax revenue.[11] Canadians and Britons may know what they pay in taxes but have little idea how their money filters through the health care system. They may not get a bill when they check out of the doctor's office or hospital—but they're paying handsomely for their care.

Consider just some of the taxes Canadians and Britons must shoulder. There's the value-added tax (VAT)—a wide-ranging sales tax of sorts added onto the value of just about every good or service as it passes through a supply chain.[12] All Canadians face a 5 percent federal VAT, called the goods and services tax.

Additionally, many provinces have chosen to adopt some form of a provincial sales tax (PST), generally around 8 percent. In provinces with their own PST, the two taxes are blended into the harmonized sales tax, which usually amounts to 13 percent overall. New Brunswick and Newfoundland residents face a 15 percent VAT.[13]

Great Britain has broadly higher income tax rates than does the United States.[14] And each Canadian province forces at least some of its residents to pay double-digit income tax rates. Manitoba taxes its residents' first dollar of income at 10.8 percent![15]

In the United States, only California maintains an income tax rate north of 10 percent—and only on individuals making more than $286,000. This "temporary" millionaires' tax passed as a ballot initiative in 2012 but has since been extended to 2030.[16]

In 2015, taxes made up just 26 percent of the U.S. GDP. In Canada and the United Kingdom, taxes accounted for closer to 35 percent of GDP.[17]

The tax burden is higher in these countries because single-payer health care is so expensive. According to the Fraser Institute, single

Canadians paid an average of C$4,544 in taxes for health care in 2019. That number jumps to C$13,163 for childless couples. The addition of a single child causes that burden to rise to C$13,208. And the average family of four pays just over C$13,300 in taxes for health care.[18]

Canadian health care taxes are on the rise. Since 1997, they've risen close to 75 percent for childless couples, and close to 70 percent for the average family of four. Single parents with two children have seen their health care tax burden rise nearly 80 percent over that same period.[19]

Health costs are growing faster than the cost of just about everything else Canadians purchase. As the Fraser report notes, "Between 1997 and 2019, the cost of public health care insurance for the average Canadian family increased 3.2 times as fast as the cost of food, 2.1 times as fast as the cost of clothing, 1.8 times as fast as the cost of shelter, and 1.7 times faster than average income."[20]

In Britain, meanwhile, the NHS costs more than £5,000 per household each year. That per household cost is up 75 percent since 2000.[21] And this figure will likely climb sharply. A report from two British think tanks determined that every British household would need to pay £2,000 more each year to keep the NHS running as the country's population ages.[22]

We've seen the toll that staffing shortages take on patients in the United Kingdom. Addressing those shortages would be expensive, if the NHS ever got around to doing so. According to the Commonwealth Fund, the average general practitioner salary in the United Kingdom is US$134,671. Multiply that by the 7,000 general practitioner vacancies anticipated by 2024, and the tab is a whopping $945 million.[23]

Of course, salaries aren't the only potential costs facing the NHS. The Service is so desperate to get more doctors that it recently announced it will pay British doctors working abroad more than £18,500 in "relocation support" to come back to the country. Officials are also trying to lure doctors out of retirement with special incentives.[24]

Those added costs won't be obvious to British citizens paying the bills.

The deeper problem with this arrangement is that it's the government, not individuals, who decide what everyone must pay for health care. In the United States, patients can exert at least a modicum of control over their health costs by shopping around for cheaper insurance plans, picking a lower-cost plan offered by their employers, or choosing to pay for their care directly.

When the government runs things, politicians make the decisions about how much every family must devote to health care—whether they like it or not.

THE HIDDEN COST OF WASTE

Far from being models of efficiency, the Canadian and British health care systems are rife with waste.

Here's one example: Canada doesn't have enough long-term care facilities, so seniors often end up staying in hospital beds longer than necessary—"bed-blocking"—because there's no place else for them to go.[25] As the *Edmonton Sun* reported in 2017, "At any given time, around 400 hospital beds in Alberta...are taken up by bed-ridden seniors waiting for placement in long-term care/nursing home/assisted-living facilities."[26] That, in turn, creates shortages of hospital beds.[27]

A 2015 report found that fraud could be costing the NHS more than £5 billion a year.[28] Another revealed that hospitals spend millions of pounds a year replacing crutches and wheelchairs taken by patients.[29]

The NHS is also spending £3.5 million a year on toiletries. Doctors filled more than 470,000 prescriptions for toiletries in 2017, up from just under 80,000 in 2007.[30] British taxpayers spent upward of £1.6 million to cover more than 195,000 prescriptions for

Aveeno body wash. The NHS also spent more than £220,000 on Neutrogena shampoos for dry and greasy hair.[31] It's unclear why the organization prescribes these items, which patients could easily buy at their local drugstore.

This sort of routine waste shouldn't come as a surprise. In the private sector, a competitive market puts relentless pressure on companies to cut waste and root out fraud. Government bureaucrats don't have the same incentives.

PAYING TO AVOID LONG QUEUES

Sure, the costs are high and growing, and the taxes are borderline confiscatory. But at least Canadians and Britons get free health care in return, right?

Not really. Patients in the two countries are forking over ever-greater sums on their own to actually secure the care their single-payer systems can't—or won't—provide.

In Britain, privately financed health care now accounts for more than 22 percent of national health spending, up from 16.5 percent in 2009, according to OECD data.[32]

Patients are paying out of pocket because they don't want to wait. One patient with prostate cancer told the *Daily Mail* in 2017 that he'd spent £6,900 for "very urgent" surgery after the NHS had delayed the procedure multiple times.[33]

An investigation by that same newspaper found that two-thirds of hospitals let patients pay out of pocket for things like hip and knee replacement and cataract surgeries. At the Royal Free Hospital in North London, patients paid up to £15,000 for a hip replacement. They paid up to £5,125 for cataract surgery at the Darby Teaching Hospitals, the *Daily Mail* found: "Many hospitals offer all-inclusive packages that work out significantly cheaper than charging separate fees for the operating theatre time, the consultant, and occupying a hospital bed," the paper reported.[34]

About two-thirds of Canadians carry private insurance to help them with the cost of things their single-payer system doesn't cover, like prescription drugs, vision care, dental care, rehab services, long-term care, and private rooms in hospitals. In many cases, this insurance is provided by U.S. firms like Blue Cross Blue Shield.[35]

Private insurance and out-of-pocket payments accounted for roughly 30 percent of the nation's health spending.[36] A 2016 survey found that 2.5 percent of Canadians—about 731,000 people—had to borrow money to pay for their prescription drugs.[37]

Canadians would like the ability to pay for medically necessary care on their own. According to a 2018 Ipsos poll, 76 percent of Canadians believed they should be allowed to pay privately when the wait lists get too long.[38]

That's against the law, of course. So Canadians head abroad to dodge their country's wait lists. Per SecondStreet.org, Canadian medical tourists spent C$690 million on treatments in 2017.[39] That spending doesn't show up on the country's health care ledger.

"Case Study: You Can't Always Get What You Want— Unless You're Wealthy"

Most Canadians are proud of their health care system's equity—rich and poor alike have the same government-run coverage.

That may be fine for cases of the sniffles. But when Canada's rich and famous face a serious health problem, they can't leave their homeland fast enough.

Take crooner Michael Bublé, who has called himself "very Canadian." He's part-owner of the Vancouver Giants junior hockey team and recently built a house across the street from his old elementary school, "complete with its own ice hockey rink," according to *Parade* magazine.[40]

But when Bublé's son Noah was diagnosed with liver cancer in 2016, the family didn't stay in Canada. They packed up and moved to California.[41] Three-year-old Noah underwent 18 months of treatment at Children's Hospital Los Angeles.[42]

Today, Noah is cancer free.[43] Bublé is understandably grateful for the hospital's efforts. "We just had the best doctors," he said.[44] Curiously enough, those doctors weren't in Canada.

Not everyone's story is as heartwarming as Bublé's.

In 2010, Newfoundland premier Danny Williams caused a political stir when he traveled to Mount Sinai Hospital in Florida for heart surgery. After the story broke, Williams defended his decision by claiming to NTV News that the surgery he needed was not offered in Canada.[45]

That backfired. Canadian cardiologists came out of the woodwork to make clear that Williams could have easily had his minimally invasive mitral valve surgery in Canada.[46]

Williams was defiant, telling reporters that he had "the utmost confidence in our health-care system," and that it was "a bum rap" to take his personal medical tourism as a vote of no confidence in Canadian health care.

Said Williams, "This is my heart, it's my health, it's my choice."[47]

The United States is also a refuge for Great Britain's rich and famous. In 2019, Rolling Stones front man Mick Jagger had an emergency heart valve replacement in New York.[48] As the singer was recovering, his brother Chris said, "At least [Mick] has not got to wait in line for the NHS."[49]

True enough. If only all Britons had that luxury.

Medical tourists pose slightly different problems in the United Kingdom. The European Health Insurance Card allows Britons to receive medically necessary care in other European Union countries. This program also entitles these countries to recoup the costs of treating foreign nationals.[50] In 2016, the United Kingdom paid out more than £670 million to other countries in the European Union. Britain took in less than one-tenth as much—just over £50 million—for providing care to foreign nationals.[51]

THE HIDDEN COST OF RATIONING AND DELAYS

The human costs of single-payer systems—the long waits, rationing, doctor shortages, and subpar treatment—are well established. But these horrors have economic impacts, too. Whether through lost income or needless suffering, single-payer care's mistreatment of patients imposes a financial burden on the entire nation.

The economic impact of delayed care in Canada is staggering. Many patients can't work while they wait for care; those who can often do so in a distracted or diminished capacity. Delays in care also add up for friends and family, who have to take time out of their lives to care for loved ones.

These costs add up. Waiting for care cost Canadian patients C$2.1 billion in 2018, according to the Fraser Institute. That shakes out to C$1,924 per patient—and that's only taking into account the typical 40-hour work week. Factor in the remaining 16 hours of each weekday along with the weekend, and that number climbs to C$6.3 billion, or C$5,860 per patient.[52]

"Would You Be Interested in Dying?"

Roger Foley was working as a bank manager in London, Ontario, when he was diagnosed with cerebellar ataxia in 2009.[53] There is no cure for this rare neurological disease, which has made it impossible for him to walk or feed himself.[54]

By 2010, he required home care to manage his day-to-day life.[55] Unfortunately, the care he received seemed to do more harm than good.

In August 2018, Foley filed a lawsuit against various government agencies and health care facilities, according to a report from CTV News. Among other things, the lawsuit alleged that the government-funded agency responsible for Foley's home care provided abysmal treatment.[56]

Foley claimed that staffers from the South West Local Health Integration Network were habitually negligent—that they gave him improper medication and injured him during exercises. He alleged the agency was unresponsive when he repeatedly complained.[57]

In March 2016, Foley applied for "self-directed funding," which would have allowed him to hire and coordinate a team of home care workers on his own.[58] On February 3, 2017, the Centre for Independent Living in Toronto rejected his request.[59]

Foley may not have qualified for self-directed funding, but as a terminal patient, he had another option. Under Canadian law, he was eligible for physician-assisted suicide.[60]

Foley released two audio recordings in which employees of the London Health Sciences Centre appeared to pressure him to end his life, CTV reported. In the first, recorded in September 2017, a staffer informed him that if he remained in the hospital, he would have to pay "north of $1,500 a day." The staffer went on to ask Foley if he had "interest in assisted dying."[61]

In the second recording, from January 2018, Foley described how his treatment in the hospital had left him so depressed that he'd considered ending his life. A hospital staffer replied, "Just apply to get an assisted, if you want to end your life, like you know what I mean?"[62]

Foley's story perfectly illustrates the double-edged sword of single-payer health care. When government-run health care facilities are unable to provide basic care for the most vulnerable patients, they have no choice but to ration care. In cases like Foley's, single-payer systems may determine medically assisted death to be the most prudent course of action—at least, for the state.

The University of British Columbia's Tom Koch summed up this ethical nightmare to CTV News: "When we are given the option for a rapid death rather than a complex life then we are all at risk."[63]

The Centre for Spatial Economics, an Ontario-based demographic research group, attempted to calculate the total per-patient economic cost of waiting for four different procedures. The analysis considered wages lost by patients and caregivers as well as costs to the health system, like the additional tests and scans brought on by waits.[64] The center determined the total cost of waiting for joint replacement surgery to be over C$26,000. The cost of waiting for an MRI scan was C$20,000.[65]

Another study found the "total lost economic output" generated by patients waiting for joint replacement surgery, cataract surgery, coronary artery bypass graft surgery, and MRI scans to be almost C$15 billion.[66]

Illness imposes major costs on the United Kingdom, too. One study found that the costs of absenteeism and "presenteeism"—that is, the reduced productivity of sick workers—were around £23 billion each year.[67] These costs are only exacerbated when patients have a harder time seeking treatment.

The NHS's poor-quality care also saddles the organization with hefty legal bills. The NHS spent £1.6 billion on clinical negligence claims from 2017 to 2018. That's a 50 percent increase over the previous year. And that's just for the actual claims. Toss in legal fees and the NHS bill rises to £2.2 billion. "Blunders in emergency medicine" accounted for the majority of these payments, according to the *Sun*.[68]

In 2018, the NHS made 336 payouts of more than £1 million, a 30 percent increase from the previous year. The NHS made 869 seven-figure payouts between 2015 and 2018. Almost half of those cases involved children nine or younger.[69] All told, 40 percent of clinical negligence claims made against the NHS have to do with delays in diagnosis or treatment.[70]

In response to these mounting claims, the NHS Litigation Authority says it expects to pay out £7.8 billion in clinical negligence costs—including damages and legal fees—over the next three years.[71] That's equivalent to more than one-third of Prime Minister May's "birthday present" for the NHS.

The response from NHS England has been to ban lawyers from advertising in hospitals in a bid to reduce claims.[72]

In other words, the British single-payer system's shortages and delays have led to more deaths and injuries, which then cost the British government a king's ransom to pay off. That leaves fewer funds available to pay doctors, build hospitals, and buy the latest equipment.

It's a downward spiral that is the inevitable result of any centrally planned health care system.

Add in the hidden costs of delays, pain and suffering, lower-quality care, untimely death, travel abroad, waste, and inefficiency, and suddenly the health care systems in Canada and the United Kingdom don't look so inexpensive. Nor does the U.S. system look so overpriced.

Free health care is very expensive indeed.

CHAPTER SEVEN

THE HORRORS OF SINGLE-PAYER INSURANCE—OUTCOMES

Eventually the combination of long wait times, low-quality care, overworked physicians, and barriers to treatment takes a toll on people's health. Life under single-payer insurance is more than just unpleasant—it's unhealthy.

Just ask the people running the show. One in three health care workers in the United Kingdom would not recommend their own hospital to a friend or family member, according to one survey.[1] Another poll found that one in six NHS staffers thought that personnel shortages put patients at risk.[2]

Still, single-payer health care's defenders insist that patients in countries with universal, government-run care are better off. To support their claims, they point to a host of health metrics where the United States underperforms. But these statistics are often misleading.

To understand why, let's break down the typical case against the U.S. health care system.

OVERSPENDING, UNDERPERFORMING

Single-payer advocates claim that U.S. health care is inefficient. According to the Commonwealth Foundation, "The United States spends far more on health care than other high-income countries...yet the U.S. population has poorer health than other countries."[3]

The implication is that the United States wastes inordinate amounts of money—and that governments in other countries have found ways to get better value for their patients' health care dollars.

One of the critics' favorite data points is America's poor infant mortality rate. With just under six deaths per 1,000 live births in 2014, the United States had the worst infant mortality of 11 developed countries tracked by the OECD.[4]

The CIA's World Factbook has 55 countries ahead of the United States on infant mortality. Serbia, Bosnia and Herzegovina, and Latvia all have lower infant mortality rates than the United States.[5]

Another apparent argument for single-payer systems is life expectancy. Babies born in the United States in 2017 could expect to live 80 years, according to the CIA's estimates. That puts the United States in 43rd place—more than five years behind Japan. Average life expectancy in Canada and the United Kingdom is 1.9 years and 0.8 years longer, respectively.[6]

Finally, the single-payer crowd appeals to rankings of various countries' health care systems from the likes of the World Health Organization (WHO) and the Commonwealth Fund. A popular WHO study ranks the U.S. health care system 37th out of 191 countries for "overall performance."[7] In 2017, the Commonwealth Fund put the United States 11th of 11 developed countries.[8]

Without broader context, each of these data points is an inadequate measure of the American health system. Taken together, they overlook what's best about health care in the United States—and distort information to make the U.S. system seem worse than it is.

MISLEADING METRICS

Let's turn first to infant mortality. Compared to other countries, the United States has a broader definition of what constitutes a "live birth." According to the National Institutes of Health, the United States reports "as live births more low-birth-weight babies who are at risk of dying on the first day, and then register[s] those who die as infant deaths."[9]

But in many European countries, an infant needs to meet certain height or weight requirements to be considered a "live" birth. Similarly, many countries classify infants who die within 24 hours of being born as "miscarriages," which are excluded from infant mortality calculations.[10]

Because the definition of infant mortality varies across countries, it's hardly an adequate measure of the quality of a health system. One study published by the *British Journal of Obstetrics and Gynaecology* found that directly adjusting the infant mortality rates of 12 Western European nations to align with a common definition could reduce some of those rates by up to 40 percent—and even change their rank order.[11]

America's infant mortality is so high in part because the United States has a lot of neonatal care centers dedicated to treating high-risk infants. With the exception of Sweden and Norway, the United States has the best infant mortality rate for babies born prematurely.[12]

In fact, when Canadians are faced with a difficult pregnancy, they turn to the United States for assistance. In 2007, 35-year-old Karen Jepp was pregnant with identical quadruplets. When she went into labor two months prematurely, every hospital in her hometown of Calgary was overbooked.[13]

So Jepp and her husband drove 325 miles to Great Falls, Montana—a town with a population of just under 60,000. There, at the Benefits Healthcare Hospital, she gave birth to four healthy baby girls in August 2007.[14]

Such an event is extremely rare. The chances of giving birth to identical quadruplets are one in 13 million.[15]

At the time, one American commentator quipped, "Great testimony for single-payer health care: Can't handle a C-section, can't find any room at neonatal intensive care units, has to fly mothers in labor to [the United States] just so they can bear children."[16]

"Death Panels for Sick Children"

Charlie Gard was born August 4, 2016. About a month later, his parents noticed that he could not move his head or support himself.[17] His parents took him to the doctor, where he was diagnosed with a form of mitochondrial DNA depletion syndrome (MDDS).[18]

Charlie was thought to be one of 16 babies in the world with this rare genetic disorder, which causes muscle weakness and respiratory failure. There is no known cure, and most babies born with MDDS die in infancy.[19]

Charlie was brought to Great Ormond Street Hospital in October 2016, where doctors reiterated his "bleak" prognosis.[20] But his parents wanted to fight for his life.

Dr. Michio Hirano, a neurologist at Columbia University Medical Center in New York, offered Charlie an experimental treatment called nucleoside therapy.[21] There was no guarantee it would work. But his parents wanted to give it a try. By April 2017, they had raised £1.2 million to pay for the treatment.[22]

There was just one problem. In March 2017, doctors at Great Ormond Street Hospital had begun petitioning the British government for permission to stop Charlie's life support, according to The Guardian.[23]

In the United Kingdom, it's up to the courts—not doctors and parents—to decide how to treat a sick child and when to cut off life support.[24] On April 11, 2017, a judge ruled that doctors could end Charlie's life.[25]

Thus began a legal battle that would take the Gards to the British High Court, Supreme Court, and the European Court of Human Rights. Charlie's parents petitioned for permission to bring their son to the United States for treatment. But the judiciary stonewalled them.[26]

The Gards had prominent allies in the fight for their son's life. The Vatican released a statement saying that Pope Francis prayed "that their desire to accompany and care for their own child to the end is not ignored."[27] They also offered to bring Charlie to Bambino Gesu, a Vatican-owned children's hospital, "to develop a protocol for experimental treatment for Charlie."[28] President Donald Trump said the United States would be "delighted" to help Charlie.[29]

Despite massive pushback, the British government held fast. Charlie died at a hospice on July 28, 2017, after the court denied his mother's request to bring her son home for his final hours.[30]

A year later, the British courts put another family through a similarly Kafkaesque saga. A young couple petitioned to bring their son Alfie to Bambino Gesu for treatment for his degenerative brain condition.[31] The boy was granted Italian citizenship, and Pope Francis again issued a personal appeal.[32]

But the British government refused to budge. Alfie died at Alder Hey Children's Hospital in Liverpool on April 28, 2018.[33] Even the pope is no match for the NHS's bureaucracy.

LIVING (AND DYING) IN AMERICA

Similarly—and perhaps counterintuitively—life expectancy isn't an accurate measure of the quality of a nation's health care system. That's largely because so many of the factors that influence life expectancy have nothing to do with health care. These are just the factors that drive down U.S. life expectancy.

For example, the United States has a much higher homicide rate than other developed countries. In 2016, there were 5.3 murders per 100,000 people in the United States.[34] That same year, the United Kingdom had just 1.2 murders per 100,000 people; Canada had about 1.7.[35]

Americans are also more likely to die in car accidents. According to the WHO, there were over 34,000 "road traffic deaths" in the United States in 2013, compared to just over 1,800 in the United

Kingdom and over 2,100 in Canada.[36] Per capita, the United States has nearly four times as many traffic deaths as the United Kingdom, and nearly twice as many as Canada.

The suicide rate in the United States is higher than in Canada and almost double that in the United Kingdom.[37]

Then there is America's epidemic of drug overdoses. According to the United Nations Office on Drugs and Crime, in 2015 the United States had around 246 drug-related deaths per 1 million people aged 15–64.[38]

Compare that to just under 105 per million in Canada in 2007, the most recent year for which data are available. The United Kingdom's drug-related death rate was 67 per million people aged 15–64 in 2014—again, the most recent year for which data are available.[39]

Unfortunately, drug-related deaths have only grown more common in the United States. The death rate from drug overdoses increased between 2013 and 2017 in all but three states.[40]

These statistics are disheartening. And they have serious implications for public policy. But it's hard to see how implementing single-payer health care in the United States would drive down the country's rate of murders or traffic accidents.

Even within the United States, health care doesn't correlate all that much with life expectancy. A study in the *Journal of the American Medical Association* found that life expectancy varies from 66 to 87 years in the United States, mostly because of behavioral and socioeconomic factors. Only 27 percent of the difference can be attributed to health care.[41]

Economists Robert L. Ohsfeldt and John E. Schneider have calculated that the United States has a higher life expectancy than all other OECD countries after adjusting for fatal injuries.[42]

And what about the WHO's all-encompassing health system rankings? The methodology leaves much to be desired.

One-quarter of the ranking comes from life expectancy—a metric we now know to be flawed. Another 25 percent derives from "financial fairness."[43] In other words, the WHO prizes health care systems that treat patients the same over those that treat them well.

As a result, the rankings aren't just flawed—they've stacked the deck in favor of single-payer systems.

THE BEST PLACE TO GET SICK

Ultimately, the best way to measure the quality of a country's health care system is to look at how patients fare when they get sick—when they actually need health care. On this score, the U.S. system performs quite well.

Take cancer. Cancer mortality in the United Kingdom is higher than in two-thirds of countries worldwide.[44] This is due in part to the poor quality of care patients receive. On average, NHS hospitals make three potentially fatal cancer diagnosis errors per week, according to the *Daily Mail*.[45]

Meanwhile, cancer patients in the United States are living longer than ever. Between 1991 and 2016, the cancer death rate in the United States "dropped continuously" by 27 percent, according to a study by the American Cancer Society. That's equivalent to over 2.6 million fewer cancer deaths than would have otherwise been expected over the same period.[46]

In the United Kingdom, cancer death rates have decreased just 16 percent since the early 1970s; in Canada, they've decreased by around 25 percent since 1988.[47]

One study found that U.S. cancer patients live longer than cancer patients in 10 European countries after the same diagnosis, thanks in part to the higher levels of spending on cancer care in the United States.[48] "Our study suggests that the higher-cost US system of cancer care delivery may be worth it," the authors wrote.[49]

"The Face of the Health Care Crisis in Nova Scotia"

Inez Rudderham knew something was wrong. The 33-year-old Nova Scotia mother had spent two years suffering from pelvic pain. She wasn't able to gain access to a family doctor, so she sought treatment in emergency rooms. The doctors repeatedly told her she had hemorrhoids.[50]

Finally, in May 2018, after visiting three emergency departments, she received a rectal exam. Two weeks later, she was diagnosed with stage 3 anal cancer.[51]

After multiple courses of radiation and chemotherapy, Rudderham's cancer is in remission.[52]

Rudderham and her family maintain that the Canadian health care system failed her. In April 2019, she posted an emotional video to Facebook in which she dared Nova Scotia premier Stephen McNeil "to take a meeting with me . . . look into my eyes, and tell me that there is no health-care crisis" in Nova Scotia.[53]

Through tears, Rudderham explained that radiation has left her "barren and infertile," with early-onset menopause. "This is the face of the health care crisis in Nova Scotia," she said.[54]

According to Canadian government statistics, 10 percent of Nova Scotia residents didn't have a doctor in 2016.[55] The national average is just under 16 percent.[56]

In less than three days, Rudderham's video racked up more than 2.5 million views—including one from Premier McNeil, who admitted there were problems with the health care system and agreed to meet with her.[57]

Rudderham put on a brave face for her meeting with McNeil. "I knew from the very beginning if I was given this cancer, it was for a reason," she told the CBC. "Maybe this is why."[58]

The United States had just 181 cancer deaths per 100,000 people in 2016, compared to 216 in the United Kingdom.[59] The five-year survival rate for breast cancer in the United States is 89 percent, outpacing most other developed countries. That includes Canada, which has a survival rate of 88 percent, and the United Kingdom, with its survival rate of 81 percent.[60]

PUTTING PATIENTS FIRST

These survival rates are a product of how much effort each country puts into screening and detection. According to the WHO, patients in the United States have better access to screenings for breast, cervical, and colorectal cancers than do those in Canada and the United Kingdom.[61] Cancer screening rates for adults over 50 are far higher in the United States than in Europe.[62]

Former New York City mayor Rudy Giuliani drew attention to this feature of the U.S. health care system while campaigning for president in 2007. Reflecting on being diagnosed with prostate cancer in the early twenty-first century, Giuliani boasted that he was given an 82 percent chance of surviving—much higher than "under socialized medicine."[63]

Some people criticized Giuliani, claiming it was "unfair" to compare survival rates between the two countries, since patients in the United States were more likely to be diagnosed early.[64] But that's part of his point. Prostate cancer patients fare better in the United States precisely because our health care system is more likely to catch cancer early.

This is just as true today. The five-year survival rate for Americans with "localized" or "regional" prostate cancer is nearly 100 percent, according to the American Cancer Society. The average five-year survival rate for Americans with all stages of prostate cancer is 98 percent.[65] British patients, meanwhile, have a survival rate just under 85 percent.[66]

Prostate cancer isn't the only disease where the United States outperforms other nations. Consider that the five-year survival rate for patients with early-stage colorectal cancer is 90 percent.[67] That rate drops to 71 percent once the cancer spreads to surrounding areas—and to 14 percent if it spreads throughout the body.[68] Early detection could quite literally save a patient's life.

In the United States, it is recommended that everyone 50 and older get screened for colorectal cancer.[69] In the United Kingdom, screening is not recommended for patients until they turn 55—and even then only if screening is "available in your area."[70] Unsurprisingly, the overall survival rate for colorectal cancer in the United Kingdom is just over 60 percent, about 5 percentage points lower than in the United States.[71]

U.S patients post better outcomes than their foreign counterparts on other diseases as well. The United States has a lower 30-day mortality rate for patients over the age of 45 admitted to the hospital with a heart attack or stroke than its peer countries, according to an analysis of OECD data conducted by the Kaiser Family Foundation.[72]

For every 100 patients admitted to the hospital with a heart attack in the United States, just under six die. In Canada, it's around seven patients per 100 admitted—and around eight per 100 in the United Kingdom.[73]

According to the White House Council of Economic Advisers, these survival gains are attributable to the fact that hospitals in the United States are more likely to use a wide variety of lifesaving treatments on older patients.[74] In countries with single-payer care, older patients are often declared lost causes and denied access to care.

I have some personal experience with such denials. My family hails from Canada. My mother died from colon cancer after doctors delayed her colonoscopy so younger people on the waiting list could go first.

"Even Doctors Have to Wait for Care Under Single-Payer Plans"

Not even those who work for hospitals in Canada and the United Kingdom are immune to the pernicious effects of single-payer health care when they become patients.

On March 12, 2017, Janice Joneja brought her husband, 83-year-old retired neurologist Rajinder Joneja, to the Royal Inland Hospital in Kamloops, British Columbia. According to the CBC, Dr. Joneja was experiencing chest pain but was still able to communicate effectively with a nurse.[75]

In a letter to the Minister of Health for British Columbia, Mrs. Joneja recalls her husband describing his medical history and his symptoms to a triage nurse in a "clear and concise" manner.[76] Dr. Joneja was then given two aspirin tablets without water and instructed to wait, according to the CBC.[77]

Five minutes later, he went into cardiac arrest. He died that afternoon, in the hospital where he had served since 1968.[78]

Mrs. Joneja has used her husband's death to warn of the dangers of single-payer systems. She told CTV News Vancouver that her husband's death is emblematic of the long wait times and lack of quality care Canadians face every day.[79]

"You cannot expect a physician...to come to a place like Kamloops when they spend years and years in study, and thousands in fees...it isn't a place that will attract the medical personnel," Janice said. The failure to attract specialists to places like the Royal Inland Hospital means that patients "literally...die en route" to the nearest specialty medical facility, three hours away.[80]

On April 7, 2017, the Interior Health Authority (IHA) issued a judgment in Joneja's case. According to CTV News, the IHA "determined that the appropriate protocols were followed and staff 'responded in a highly professional and skillful manner.'"[81]

Margaret Hutchon had a similar experience in her native United Kingdom. She died in 2011 after waiting nine months for a surgical procedure at a hospital on whose board of directors she once served. According to her husband, she had initially undergone stomach surgery in June 2010 and was scheduled to receive a follow-up.[82]

The *Daily Mail* reported that Hutchon's follow-up was rescheduled four times over nine months.[83] According to the *Mirror*, she finally received the surgery she'd been waiting for on March 21, 2011.[84]

She died four days later at Broomfield Hospital in Chelmsford, the Essex town where she had once served as mayor.[85]

Her husband was understandably frustrated. "I don't really know why she died. I did not get a reason from the hospital," he said.[86]

The hospital was not inclined to give him one. Per the *Daily Mail*, "Broomfield Hospital said it could not comment on individual cases."[87]

Even to their spouses, apparently.

———————————

Even compared to other countries with universal health coverage, those with true single-payer systems underperform.

A Fraser Institute study of 28 countries with universal health care found that the United Kingdom's five-year survival rates for breast, cervical, colon, and rectal cancer were all below the OECD average.[88] Canada and the United Kingdom ranked 18th and 21st, respectively, for their 30-day mortality rate for patients admitted to the hospital with hemorrhagic stroke.[89] Canadian women also suffered trauma during vaginal childbirth more frequently than any of their peers in the 19 developed countries for which Fraser had data.[90]

YOU GET WHAT YOU PAY FOR

Focus on actual health outcomes, and it's clear the United States outperforms most other countries, especially those with single-payer care. Americans are healthier because our health care system devotes more resources to the best treatments, technology, and physicians. The United States may spend more on health care than other countries, but Americans are getting the most bang for their buck.

This shouldn't come as a surprise. Markets are the most efficient way to allocate scarce resources. It makes no difference if we're dealing with something as simple as a loaf of bread or as complex as cancer treatment. To improve our health care system, we don't need to suppress the free market. We need to unleash it.

CHAPTER EIGHT

AN ALTERNATIVE VISION FOR HEALTH CARE REFORM

C learly, we need a new vision for health care in this country—one that will provide affordable, high-quality health
care to all. Thus far, we've waded through loads of evidence
that single-payer care, or stepping-stone approaches to it, will not
deliver that vision.

Market principles can—if we let them.

WHO NEEDS SINGLE-PAYER HEALTH CARE?

Medicare for All has two chief selling points. The first is universal
coverage. The second is its supposedly lower cost. But as we've seen,
access to coverage does not equal access to care. And single-payer
care is very costly, in both financial and human terms.

Let's take a step back. Is universal coverage really what we
should be aiming for, especially if it'll cost taxpayers more than
$3 trillion a year, lead to long waits and rationed care, and require
the wholesale restructuring of no less than one-sixth of the U.S.
economy?

Most Americans already have health insurance. For some, that coverage may not be perfect. But it's a lot easier, and cheaper, to improve the coverage people have than to create a new health care system out of whole cloth.

The United States isn't that far away from universal coverage. In 2017, 28 million people were uninsured.[1] That's less than 10 percent of the population. Drawing them into existing coverage arrangements shouldn't be that hard.

According to Joseph Antos and James C. Capretta of the American Enterprise Institute, 19 million of those folks—more than two-thirds—are eligible for publicly subsidized or employer-sponsored insurance but haven't enrolled.[2] Getting them covered may be as simple as asking them to sign up.

Another two million people "are ineligible for employer coverage and for premium credits" under Obamacare. But they're wealthier than the average American—they come from families with incomes over $100,000 a year.[3] It's hard to justify publicly subsidized health coverage for people whose incomes are 60 percent higher—at a minimum—than the national median.[4]

Ultimately, Antos and Capretta found, "only 2.5 million people—or less than 1 percent of the total population—were in the U.S. legally, had low incomes, and did not have ready access to an insurance plan."[5]

It would be cheaper for the federal government to give each of these 2.5 million uninsured a million dollars than to implement Medicare for All.

A MARKET-BASED ALTERNATIVE

We don't need a government overhaul of the health care system to provide affordable insurance to 1 percent of the population—or to ease the health cost burden the other 99 percent face.

In fact, we need the opposite. Market principles have yielded better quality and lower costs in just about every sector of the economy. The two primary exceptions are those where government's hand is most intrusive: education and health care.

Foes of markets in health care tend to raise the specter of insurers denying coverage to the sick or raising rates so high that the poor won't be able to afford insurance or care.

A successful market-based reform plan can restore affordability and choice in health care—and maintain the consumer protections Americans have come to expect.

My vision for health care reform achieves both of those goals by putting patients in control and leveraging the power of competition.

CLEAR THE OBSTACLES

Any successful market-based reform effort will begin by fully repealing Obamacare.

The Affordable Care Act was anything but market-based—and has been anything but a success. Insurance is pricier than ever; deductibles are higher than ever. Consumers have seen their coverage choices dwindle.

Average monthly premiums for the benchmark health insurance plan for a 40-year-old individual increased 75 percent between 2014 and 2019.[6] Nearly four in 10 counties nationwide had only one choice of insurer in 2019.[7]

Obamacare's costly mandates, regulations, and taxes are to blame. Things like guaranteed issue, which requires insurers to accept all comers, and community rating, which caps the prices they can charge, ensured that premiums overall would rise. Its 10 essential benefits mandates forced consumers to purchase coverage for services and procedures they may not have wanted. And its new taxes on insurers, medical devices, and drugs were simply passed on to ordinary Americans in the form of higher prices.

Sweeping those mandates, regulations, and taxes away would immediately reduce the cost of insurance—and of care.

Republicans started that process in December 2017, by enacting a tax reform law that set Obamacare's penalty for going without insurance coverage to zero, effective January 1, 2019. But lawmakers have a long way to go.

LEVEL THE PLAYING FIELD

Congress must then equalize the tax treatment of health insurance between employers and individuals.

For more than 70 years, employers have been able to offer health benefits tax-free. That policy started during World War II, when employers used such benefits to attract and retain workers without running afoul of federal wage controls. The tax exemption survived the war—and established employer-sponsored insurance as the cornerstone of the U.S. health care system.

Exempting health benefits from tax is costly. The exclusion deprives the U.S. Treasury of about $280 billion each year.[8]

It also drives up health spending. One dollar of untaxed health benefits is worth more than a taxed dollar of wages. So many workers prefer to receive their marginal compensation in the form of untaxed benefits. And they put those additional benefit dollars to use, by consuming more care than they might if they had to use taxed dollars to pay for it.

Further, employer-sponsored insurance insulates patients from the true cost of their care. They have to look at their pay stub to see how much of their compensation goes toward health care—rather than writing a check each month, as they might for other forms of insurance.

Economics tells us that if we subsidize something, we get more of it. Our tax code subsidizes spending on employer-sponsored health benefits, so we get more of it. As the Hamilton Project at the Brookings Institution has put it, "Benefits have made up an increasingly large share of compensation, [while] wage growth has lagged."[9]

Health care providers have been more than happy to take those tax-advantaged dollars from patients and their employers. It's no wonder that prices for health care have historically increased at a rate higher than general inflation.

Capping the tax exclusion for employer-sponsored insurance would rein in spending and put cash in the pockets of working Americans. The deduction could reasonably be capped at $8,000 for individuals and $20,000 for families. Those caps could be raised each year at the rate of inflation plus 1 percent.

EMPOWER CONSUMERS

Almost half of health expenses were paid out of pocket in 1965, when employer-sponsored insurance was still relatively new, and Medicare and Medicaid were in their infancy.[10] Today, only 11 percent of health expenses come out of patients' pockets.[11]

It's no wonder, then, that so many Americans expect "someone else" to cover their health care for them. The best way to change this mindset—and to slow federal health care spending—is to build a health care system centered on patients as consumers.

Expanding the use of health savings accounts (HSAs) would do just that. HSAs allow individuals to save money tax-free that can later be used to cover medical expenses.

Patients are generally more careful stewards of their own money than of their insurer's or employer's. HSAs inject some consumerism and price-consciousness into the health care marketplace.

Currently, only those enrolled in high-deductible health plans are eligible to contribute to HSAs. Why not make them available to everyone?

Other tweaks could make HSAs even more powerful. For example, Congress could change the tax code to allow people to use HSA dollars to pay insurance premiums, which they're currently barred from doing.[12] It could also authorize patients on Medicare to deposit money into the accounts. That's also against the law at present.

In addition, lawmakers could loosen the restrictions on what patients can contribute to HSAs. In 2019, HSA contributions were capped at $3,500 for individuals and $7,000 for families.[13] Michael Cannon of the Cato Institute has proposed letting people contribute the equivalent of what their employer would have otherwise spent on employer-sponsored insurance. His proposal would cap contributions at $8,000 for individuals and $16,000 for families.[14]

Cannon argues that so-called "large HSAs" would put pressure on employers to increase wages instead of offering health coverage.

Alternatively, the HSA contribution cap could be set to match the cap for individual retirement accounts. In 2019, IRA contributions were limited to $6,000 for individuals under age 50 and $7,000 for those 50 and older.[15]

UNLEASH COMPETITION

Repealing Obamacare is a necessary but insufficient step toward bringing about a competitive insurance market. States and the federal government had scores of mandates on the books well before Obamacare—around 2,000 nationwide, according to one estimate.[16]

Those benefit mandates aren't free. Insurers have to raise premiums to cover the cost of every benefit or procedure the state directs them to include gratis in their policies. One study found that each additional benefit mandate can raise monthly premiums by up to 5 percent.[17] Over time, mandated benefits have driven up the cost of health insurance anywhere from 20 percent to 50 percent.[18]

Mandates also discourage competition. When states micromanage what each policy must cover, they make it harder for insurers to differentiate themselves. Consumers, meanwhile, have little incentive to shop around; the state has already made their choices for them. New insurers have little incentive to enter the market.

An army of consumers entering the market with pretax dollars in their HSAs, each with different preferences, might change that state of affairs. Some might demand bare-bones policies. Others would be looking for gold-plated plans. Insurers would likely be thrilled to come up with health plans to meet those demands.

The Trump administration has tried to boost competition in the health care marketplace through executive action. In October 2017, the president signed an executive order to that effect—the appropriately named "Promoting Healthcare Choice and Competition Across the United States."[19]

Among other things, the order rolled back Obama-era restrictions on short-term, limited-duration insurance, an affordable alternative to the plans for sale on the exchanges. Short-term plans can last up to a year, are renewable for up to three years, and do not have to cover all of Obamacare's essential health benefits. As a result, the average short-term plan costs about 70 percent less than an unsubsidized Obamacare plan.[20]

Sadly, many liberal politicians have made potential buyers skeptical of these plans by describing them as "junk insurance." Some states have banned them, arguing that they sabotage the conventional insurance market. They would apparently prefer that consumers have fewer affordable health insurance choices.

Any market-oriented health plan should also take aim at other regulations that keep health care expensive. For example, states should relax restrictions on the types of work that highly skilled—and less expensive—nurse practitioners and physician assistants can perform.

Similarly, states should remove restrictions on retail clinics. These small, walk-in facilities operate out of supermarkets and pharmacies and are primarily staffed by NPs and PAs.[21] They're much more affordable than the clinical status quo. According to research published in the *Journal of the American Medical Association* in 2018, the average "low-severity emergency room visit" cost $422 out of pocket; taking care of that problem at a standard retail clinic ran just $37.[22]

States could also repeal certificate of need laws that give incumbent hospitals and clinical facilities virtual veto power over the entry of new competitors.

Increased use of telemedicine could help lower health costs further. Recent research conducted by Regence, an administrator of Blue Cross Blue Shield plans across the Pacific Northwest, found that the average telehealth visit can save the average patient about $100.[23]

Many states restrict the delivery of care over the internet or via services like Skype. Wiping away those regulations would save money and improve access to care, particularly for patients who live in remote areas.

Then there are the onerous federal mandates that require providers to use electronic health records. They must go. These mandates have saddled medical practices with huge capital and compliance costs, often for software that doesn't work. They've also cut the amount of time doctors can spend actually treating patients.

Finally, federal lawmakers should push the states to reform their tort law systems. Health care providers routinely order more tests and procedures than necessary out of an abundance of caution, because they're afraid of being sued for medical malpractice. This practice of defensive medicine adds tens, if not hundreds, of billions of dollars to America's health bill each year.[24]

Capping non-economic damages in medical malpractice cases could reduce health costs by between 5 percent and 9 percent, according to an authoritative study from the Department of Health and Human Services.[25] That's equivalent to billions of dollars in potential savings—savings patients would see in the form of lower premiums and prices.

PROTECTING THOSE WITH PREEXISTING CONDITIONS

Market-friendly health reform can also deliver affordable health care to those with preexisting conditions.

It's important to remember that fewer people have preexisting conditions than fans of single-payer health care would have us think. In the years leading up to the passage of Obamacare, insurers denied coverage to just one in seven people because of a preexisting condition.[26] The Kaiser Family Foundation estimates that fewer than 3 in 10 Americans under 65 have preexisting conditions that would leave them unable to buy insurance on the individual market absent Obamacare's regulations.[27]

Prohibiting insurers from denying sick people coverage is a noble goal. It's also an expensive one.

Obamacare's individual mandate was meant to counterbalance

the costs associated with the coverage guarantee. Premiums from the young and healthy, who are unlikely to actually use their insurance benefits, would help offset the costs associated with treating older, sicker patients.

This elegant theory didn't work out in practice. Millions of people opted to pay the tax for going without coverage instead of paying premiums that were many times greater.

Worse, many people waited until they got sick to sign up for coverage. That left an insurance pool disproportionately composed of high-cost patients. Insurers had little choice but to raise premiums across the board to stay solvent.

There's a better way to ensure coverage for everyone. Insurers should be required to cover anyone who maintains continuous coverage from year to year, without raising their premiums if they get sick.

The combination of expanded HSAs and a competitive insurance market should make it easy for every American to maintain coverage.

A continuous coverage requirement will incentivize young and healthy people to buy and hold insurance, since they'll want to lock in lower premiums while they can. That will ensure a steady flow of premiums into the insurance risk pool and prevent the unintended spike in cost that occurs when people only sign up for coverage after getting sick.

To further offset the cost of covering everyone, insurers should be able to charge the old five times what they charge the young, as opposed to the three-to-one ratio allowed by Obamacare. A five-to-one ratio more closely matches the actual claims costs of the old and the young.

Finally, for those who truly cannot secure affordable coverage because of preexisting conditions or health status, Congress must provide robust funding for a state-based network of high-risk pools.

Such pools segregate the sickest people from the rest of the population. That offers several benefits. First, it makes the broader insurance market more actuarially sound. Insurers can predict with greater accuracy the health expenses of people who are in average health. That allows them to keep premiums stable and affordable for the majority of the population.

Second, high-risk pools prevent healthy people from paying more than their fair share to offset the medical expenses of those with preexisting conditions, whose expenses may be high but are often predictable. States are better off paying them directly than destroying their insurance markets as part of a misguided effort to socialize costs across the entire insurance pool.

REIN IN ENTITLEMENT SPENDING

No market-oriented health plan is complete unless it addresses our nation's reckless entitlement spending. In 2017, just under 40 percent of Americans got their health insurance through Medicare and Medicaid, which accounted for 20 percent and 17 percent of national health expenditures, respectively.[28]

Spending in these programs has grown steadily and is not slowing down. Medicare spending is projected to hit $1.4 trillion in 2027. Medicaid spending isn't far behind; it will reach $992 billion the same year.[29]

Medicaid is also growing at an unsustainable rate, thanks in part to its joint state-federal payment structure and the costly expansion of the program brought on by Obamacare. Currently, the government matches every dollar states spend on Medicaid with additional funding. As such, states are incentivized to spend more on the program, even at the expense of other priorities like education or transportation.

Both of these problems can be solved by changing the way Medicaid is administered. First, federal Medicaid funding should be sent to the states as block grants. That will remove the incentive for states to increase spending on Medicaid just to get more "matching" funds. Block grants also allow states to structure their Medicaid programs in ways that meet the unique needs of their populations.

We can start reforming Medicare by raising the eligibility age to 67. When Medicare launched in 1964, average U.S. life expectancy was just over 70 years.[30] So the federal government could count on paying for health benefits for just over five years.

Life expectancy today is nearly a decade longer. But seniors are still eligible to receive Medicare at 65.[31] That means taxpayers are on the hook for seniors' medical expenses for an average of about 15 years—one-fifth of the average person's life. No wonder the program is in financial trouble.

Further, seniors should be encouraged to shop around for Medicare plans, just as everyone else would under this market-based reform plan. This idea isn't radical. Many Medicare beneficiaries already shop for coverage. Around one in four pay for private "Medigap" plans to supplement their Medicare benefits or to gain access to doctors who refuse to treat Medicare patients.[32]

Medicare Advantage—which gives private insurers the flexibility to design and administer Medicare plans—is incredibly popular with seniors. We can capitalize on Medicare Advantage's success by giving seniors vouchers to put toward Medicare plans. Seniors can supplement these vouchers with their own money, including anything they've saved in an HSA.

LET'S TRY MARKETS—FOR THE FIRST TIME

It's said that the definition of insanity is doing the same thing repeatedly but expecting different results. For almost a century, the United States has given government more and more control over the health care system. The results speak for themselves—prices and spending have gone through the roof, and Americans are increasingly dissatisfied.

Single-payer advocates think that giving government complete control of the U.S. health care system is the solution. This book's in-depth look at the single-payer systems in Canada and the United Kingdom proves just how insane that is.

To solve America's health care crisis, let's try an approach we've avoided for decades—one that relies less on government, and more on market principles.

NOTES

FOREWORD

1 "Marketplace Average Benchmark Premiums," Kaiser Family Foundation, October 2018, https://www.kff.org/health-reform/state-indicator. marketplace-average-benchmark-premiums, "Timeframe: 2014–2019."

2 Tami Luhby, "Fact Check: Are Obamacare's Deductible's More than $7,000?," CNN, April 2, 2019, https://www.cnn.com/2019/04/01/politics/fact-check-obamacare-deductibles/index.html.

3 Seto J. Bagdoyan, "Medicare: Actions Needed to Better Manage Fraud Risks," U.S. Government Accountability Office, July 17, 2018, https://www.gao.gov/assets/700/693156.pdf; "The 2019 OASDI Trustees Report," Social Security, 2019, https://www.ssa.gov/oact/TR/2019/index.html.

INTRODUCTION: "MEDICARE FOR ALL" MANIA SWEEPS THE POLITICAL LEFT

1 Nate Silver, "Was the Democratic Primary a Close Call or a Landslide?," *FiveThirtyEight*, July 26, 2016, https://fivethirtyeight.com/features/was-the-democratic-primary-a-close-call-or-a-landslide.

2 Gabriel Debenedetti, "Sanders, Clinton Clash After His New 'Medicare for All' Plan," *Politico*, January 17, 2016, https://www.politico.com/story/2016/01/bernie-sanders-health-plan.

3 Will Cabaniss, "George Will Describes Bernie Sanders' Soviet Union Honeymoon," *Politifact*, August 12, 2015, https://www.politifact.com/punditfact/statements/2015/aug/12/george-will/george-will-reminds-readers-about-bernie-sanders-u.

4 "Public Opinion on Single-Payer, National Health Plans, and Expanding Access to Medicare Coverage," Kaiser Family Foundation, September 12, 2019, https://www.kff.org/slideshow/public-opinion-on-single-payer-national-health-plans-and-expanding-access-to-medicare-coverage, fig. 4.

5 Medicare for All Act of 2017, S. 1804, 115th Cong. (2017); Medicare for All Act of 2019, S. 1129, 116th Congress (2019).

6 Medicare for All Act of 2017, S. 1804.

7   Justin McCarthy, "Seven in 10 Maintain Negative View of U.S. Healthcare System," Gallup, January 14, 2019, https://news.gallup.com/poll/245873/seven-maintain-negative-view-healthcare-system.aspx.

8   McCarthy, "Seven in 10."

9   Jeffrey M. Jones and R.J. Reinhart, "Americans Remain Dissatisfied with Healthcare Costs," Gallup, November 28, 2018, https://news.gallup.com/poll/245054/americans-remain-dissatisfied-healthcare-costs.aspx.

10 Gary Claxton, Matthew Rae, Larry Levitt, and Cynthia Cox, "How Have Healthcare Prices Grown in the U.S. Over Time?," Kaiser Family Foundation, May 8, 2018, https://www.healthsystemtracker.org/chart-collection/how-have-healthcare-prices-grown-in-the-u-s-over-time/#item-the-price-of-office-visits-has-risen-consistently-since-2003.

11 "2019 Employer Health Benefits Survey," Kaiser Family Foundation, September 25, 2019, https://www.kff.org/report-section/ehbs-2019-section-1-cost-of-health-insurance, section 1: Cost of Health Insurance, and https://www.kff.org/report-section/ehbs-2019-summary-of-findings, Summary of Findings.

12 "Nominal Wage Tracker," Economic Policy Institute, accessed May 28, 2019, https://www.epi.org/nominal-wage-tracker.

13 "HHS Report: Average Health Insurance Premiums Doubled Since 2013," U.S. Department of Health and Human Services, May 23, 2017, https://www.hhs.gov/about/news/2017/05/23/hhs-report-average-health-insurance-premiums-doubled-2013.html.

14 Rachel Garfield, Kendal Orgera, and Anthony Damico, "The Uninsured and the ACA: A Primer—Key Facts about Health Insurance and the Uninsured Amidst Changes to the Affordable Care Act," Kaiser Family Foundation, January 25, 2019, https://www.kff.org/report-section/the-uninsured-and-the-aca-a-primer-key-facts-about-health-insurance-and-the-uninsured-amidst-changes-to-the-affordable-care-act-how-many-people-are-uninsured.

15 "Medicaid Enrollment Changes Following the ACA," MACPAC, accessed May 28, 2019, https://www.macpac.gov/subtopic/medicaid-enrollment-changes-following-the-aca.

16 Rachana Pradhan, "Number of Uninsured Americans Rises for the First Time Since Obamacare," Politico, September 10, 2019, https://www.politico.com/story/2019/09/10/health-insurance-rate-1719381.

17 "Health Insurance Exchanges 2019 Open Enrollment Report," Centers for Medicare & Medicaid Services, March 25, 2019, https://www.cms.gov/newsroom/fact-sheets/health-insurance-exchanges-2019-open-enrollment-report.

CHAPTER ONE: HEALTH CARE IS NOT A RIGHT

1   U.N. General Assembly, Resolution 217A, Universal Declaration of Human Rights, article 25 (December 10, 1948), https://www.un.org/en/universal-declaration-human-rights.

2   Julie Rovner, "Kennedy's Lasting Devotion to Healthcare for All," NPR, August 26, 2009, https://www.npr.org/templates/story/story.php?storyId=112242975.

3   Robert Pear, "Clinton's Health Plan: The Overview; Congress Is Given Clinton Proposal for Healthcare," New York Times, October 28, 1993, https://www.

nytimes.com/1993/10/28/us/clinton-s-health-plan-overview-congress-given-clinton-proposal-for-health-care.html.

4 Scott Wilson and Ovetta Wiggins, "Obama Defends Health-Care Law, Calling Health Insurance 'A Right,'" *Washington Post*, September 26, 2013, https://www.washingtonpost.com/politics/obama-defends-health-care-law-calling-health-insurance-a-right.

5 Bernie Sanders, "Bernie Sanders: Why We Need Medicare for All," *New York Times*, September 13, 2017, https://www.nytimes.com/2017/09/13/opinion/bernie-sanders-medicare-single-payer.html; Matthew Yglesias, "Joe Biden Is Leading the 2020 Polls: Here's What He Thinks About Policy," *Vox*, December 18, 2018, https://www.vox.com/policy-and-politics/2018/12/18/18143882/joe-biden-2020-economic-policy.

6 Sean Illing, "I Think Healthcare Is a Right: I Asked an Expert to Tell Me Why I'm Wrong," *Vox*, June 30, 2017, https://www.vox.com/policy-and-politics/2017/6/30/15879702/health-care-capitalism-free-market-socialism-single-payer.

7 Michael Winship, "An 'Exciting but Dangerous Moment' for Medicare for All," *Common Dreams*, February 20, 2019, https://www.commondreams.org/views/2019/02/20/exciting-dangerous-moment-medicare-all.

8 Michelle Chen, "The Human-Rights Agenda Underlying the 2019 Medicare for All Bill," *The Nation*, March 20, 2019, https://www.thenation.com/article/healthcare-medicare-human-rights.

9 Chen, "Human-Rights Agenda."

10 U.S. Declaration of Independence (1776), https://www.archives.gov/founding-docs/declaration-transcript.

11 U.S. Const. art. I, https://www.archives.gov/founding-docs/bill-of-rights-transcript.

12 Schenck v. United States, 249 U.S. 47 (1919), https://www.law.cornell.edu/supremecourt/text/249/47.

13 U.S. Const. amend. XIV, § 1, https://www.law.cornell.edu/constitution-conan/amendment-14/section-1/the-right-to-travel.

14 Laura Donnelly, "NHS Provokes Fury with Indefinite Surgery Ban for Smokers and Obese," *Telegraph*, October 17, 2017, https://www.telegraph.co.uk/news/2017/10/17/nhs-provokes-fury-indefinite-surgery-ban-smokers-obese.

15 Bruce Cheadle, "Universal Healthcare Much Loved Among Canadians, Monarchy Less Important: Poll," *Globe and Mail*, November 25, 2012, https://www.theglobeandmail.com/news/national/universal-health-care-much-loved-among-canadians-monarchy-less-important-poll/article5640454.

16 Amanda Coletta, "Canada's Healthcare System Is a Point of National Pride: But a Study Shows It's at Risk of Becoming Outdated," *Washington Post*, February 23, 2018, https://www.washingtonpost.com/news/worldviews/wp/2018/02/23/canadas-health-care-system-is-a-point-of-national-pride-but-a-study-shows-it-might-be-stalled.

17 Richard Wike, "5 Ways Americans and Europeans Are Different," Pew Research, April 19, 2016, https://www.pewresearch.org/fact-tank/2016/04/19/5-ways-americans-and-europeans-are-different.

18 "Philosophy of Rugged Individualism," UVA Miller Center, accessed March

19, 2019, https://millercenter.org/the-presidency/educational-resources/philosophy-of-rugged-individualism.

19 Holly Van Hare, "Fast Food Meals Are 'Calorie Capped' by British Government," *Chicago Tribune*, January 16, 2018, https://www.chicagotribune.com/dining/sns-dailymeal-1866879-healthy-eating-fast-food-meals-calorie-cap-british-government-011618-20180116-story.html.

20 Nick Triggle, "Soft Drink Sugar Tax Starts, but Will It Work?," *BBC News*, April 6, 2018, https://www.bbc.com/news/health-43659124.

21 Erin Allday, "Berkeley's Sugary Soda Consumption Plummeted after Tax, Study Says," *San Francisco Chronicle*, February 21, 2019, https://www.sfchronicle.com/bayarea/article/Berkeley-s-sugary-soda-consumption-plummeted-13634925.php.

22 Caitlin Dewey, "Why Chicago's Soda Tax Fizzled after Two Months—and What It Means for the Anti-Soda Movement," *Washington Post*, October 10, 2017, https://www.washingtonpost.com/news/wonk/wp/2017/10/10/why-chicagos-soda-tax-fizzled-after-two-months-and-what-it-means-for-the-anti-soda-movement.

23 Anna Tuchman, Stephan Seiler, and Song Yao, "The Impact of Soda Taxes: Pass-Through, Tax Avoidance, and Nutritional Effects," Kellogg School of Management, 2019, https://www.kellogg.northwestern.edu/faculty/Research/ResearchDetail?guid=8811c8d4-bbe6-11e7-9da1-0242ac140003.

CHAPTER TWO: SINGLE-PAYER PROPOSALS UNDER CONSIDERATION

1   Medicare for All Act of 2019, H.R. 1384, 116th Cong. (2019).

2   Mary Ellen McIntire, "Bernie Sanders' New Medicare for All Bill Would Cover Some Long-Term Care," *Roll Call*, April 10, 2019, https://www.rollcall.com/news/congress/bernie-sanders-new-single-payer-bill-would-cover-some-long-term-care.

3   Medicare for All Act of 2019, H.R. 1384, Cosponsors.

4   "Key Design Components and Considerations for Establishing a Single-Payer Health Care System," Congressional Budget Office, May 2019, https://www.cbo.gov/system/files/2019-05/55150-singlepayer.pdf, pp. 3, 18.

5   Medicare for All Act of 2019, H.R. 1384; Medicare for All Act of 2017, S. 1804.

6   Katie Keith, "Unpacking the House Medicare-for-All Bill," *Health Affairs*, March 3, 2019, https://www.healthaffairs.org/do/10.1377/hblog20190302.150578/full.

7   Pramila Jayapal, "Medicare for All Act of 2019," Pramila Jayapal, Congresswoman for WA-07, accessed March 25, 2019, https://jayapal.house.gov/wp-content/uploads/2019/02/Medicare-for-All-Act-of-2019_Summary-002.pdf, p. 1.

8   Juliette Cubanski, Anthony Damico, Tricia Neuman, and Gretchen Jacobson, "Sources of Supplemental Coverage Among Medicare Beneficiaries in 2016," Kaiser Family Foundation, November 28, 2018, https://www.kff.org/medicare/issue-brief/sources-of-supplemental-coverage-among-medicare-beneficiaries-in-2016.

9   "Medicare Costs at a Glance," Medicare.gov, 2019, https://www.medicare.gov/your-medicare-costs/medicare-costs-at-a-glance.

10 "Out-of-Pocket Expenditure (% of Current Health Expenditure)," World Bank,

accessed May 24, 2019, https://data.worldbank.org/indicator/SH.XPD.OOPC. CH.ZS.

11 "Out-of-Pocket Expenditure."

12 Medicare for All Act of 2019, H.R. 1384, § 107(a); Medicare for All Act of 2019, S. 1129, § 107(a).

13 Edward R. Berchick, Emily Hood, and Jessica C. Barnett, "Health Insurance Coverage in the United States: 2017," U.S. Census Bureau, September 2018, https://www.census.gov/content/dam/Census/library/publications/2018/ demo/p60-264.pdf, table 1; "An Overview of Medicare," Kaiser Family Foundation, February 13, 2019, https://www.kff.org/medicare/issue-brief/an-overview-of-medicare.

14 "Medicare Managed Care Tracker," Kaiser Family Foundation, accessed April 30, 2019, https://www.kff.org/medicaid/state-indicator/total-medicaid-mc-en rollment/?currentTimeframe=0&sortModel=%7B%22colId%22:%22Location% 22,%22sort%22:%22asc%22%7D.

15 Ashley Kirzinger, Cailey Muñana, and Mollyann Brodie, "KFF Health Tracking Poll—January 2019: The Public on Next Steps for the ACA and Proposals to Expand Coverage," Kaiser Family Foundation, January 23, 2019, https://www.kff.org/health-reform/poll-finding/kff-health-tracking-poll-january-2019.

16 Medicare for All Act of 2017, S. 1804.

17 Medicare for All Act of 2019, H.R. 1384, § 1001.

18 Amanda Michelle Gomez, "Here's What the Democrats' New Medicare for All Bill Would Do," Think Progress, February 26, 2019, https://thinkprogress. org/heres-what-the-democrats-new-medicare-for-all-bill-would-do-c82aba05861d.

19 Amy Goldstein, "HHS Failed to Heed Many Warnings that HealthCare. gov Was in Trouble," *Washington Post*, February 23, 2016, https://www. washingtonpost.com/national/health-science/hhs-failed-to-heed-many-warnings-that-healthcaregov-was-in-trouble/2016/02/22/dd344e7c-d67e-11e5-9823-02b905009f99_story.html.

20 Sarah Kliff, "Bernie Sanders's Medicare-for-All Plan, Explained," *Vox*, April 10, 2019, https://www.vox.com/2019/4/10/18304448/bernie-sanders-medicare-for-all.

21 Charles Blahous, "The Costs of a National Single-Payer Healthcare System," Mercatus working paper, George Mason University, July 2018, https://www. mercatus.org/system/files/blahous-costs-medicare-mercatus-working-paper-v1_1.pdf, p. 10.

22 Keith, "Unpacking the House Medicare-for-All Bill."

23 Katie Keith and Timothy Jost, "Unpacking the Sanders Medicare-for-All Bill," *Health Affairs*, September 14, 2017, https://www.healthaffairs.org/do/10.1377/ hblog20170914.061996/full.

24 National Nurses United and the Sanders Institute, "Medicare for All Vs. All the Healthcare That Each Can Afford," *Sanders Institute*, no date, https:// www.sandersinstitute.com/blog/medicare-for-all-vs-all-the-healthcare-that-each-can-afford.

25 Gigi Moreno, Emma van Eijndhoven, Jennifer Benner, and Jeffrey Sullivan, "The Long-Term Impact of Price Controls in Medicare Part D," *Forum for*

Health Economics & Policy 20, no. 2 (2017), https://doi.org/10.1515/fhep-2016-0011.

26   Rexford E. Santerre and John A. Vernon, "A Cost-Benefit Analysis of Drug Price Controls in the U.S.," AEI-Brookings Joint Center for Regulatory Studies, October 2004, https://www.researchgate.net/publication/46454282_A_Cost-Benefit_Analysis_of_Drug_Price_Controls_in_the_US.

27   Charles Blahous, "The Winners and Losers of Medicare for All," *Economics 21*, May 22, 2019, https://economics21.org/medicare-for-all-winners-and-losers.

28   John Holahan, Lisa Clemans-Cope, Matthew Buettgens, Melissa Favreault, Linda J. Blumberg, and Siyabonga Ndwandwe, "The Sanders Single-Payer Health Care Plan: The Effect on National Health Expenditures and Federal and Private Spending," Urban Institute, May 2016, https://www.urban.org/sites/default/files/publication/80486/200785-The-Sanders-Single-Payer-Health-Care-Plan.pdf.

29   "The Budget and Economic Outlook: 2019 to 2029," Congressional Budget Office, January 2019, https://www.cbo.gov/system/files?file=2019-03/54918-Outlook-3.pdf, table 1-1.

30   "The Budget and Economic Outlook," table 1-1 (individual and corporate income taxes over the next decade total $27.1 trillion).

31   Bernie Sanders, "Options to Finance Medicare for All," Bernie Sanders, U.S. Senator for Vermont, accessed May 6, 2019, https://www.sanders.senate.gov/download/options-to-finance-medicare-for-all?inline=file.

32   Chad Reese, "Medicare for All: $32 Trillion in New Costs or $2 Trillion in Savings?" Mercatus, August 9, 2018, https://www.mercatus.org/bridge/commentary/medicare-all-32-trillion-new-costs-or-2-trillion-savings.

33   Glenn Kessler, "Democrats Seize on Cherry-Picked Claim That 'Medicare-for-All' Would Save $2 Trillion," *Washington Post*, August 7, 2018, https://www.washingtonpost.com/news/fact-checker/wp/2018/08/07/democrats-seize-on-cherry-picked-claim-that-medicare-for-all-will-save-2-trillion.

34   Austin Frakt, "Is Medicare for All the Answer to Sky-High Administrative Costs?," *New York Times*, October 15, 2018, https://www.nytimes.com/2018/10/15/upshot/is-medicare-for-all-the-answer-to-sky-high-administrative-costs.html; Boards of Trustees, Federal Hospital Insurance and Federal Supplementary Medical Insurance Trust Funds, "2018 Annual Report," Washington, D.C., June 5, 2018, https://www.cms.gov/Research-Statistics-Data-and-Systems/Statistics-Trends-and-Reports/ReportsTrustFunds/Downloads/TR2018.pdf.

35   Bagdoyan, "Medicare: Actions Needed."

36   Juliette Cubanski, Tricia Neuman, and Meredith Freed, "The Facts on Medicare Spending and Financing," Kaiser Family Foundation, August 20, 2019, https://www.kff.org/medicare/issue-brief/the-facts-on-medicare-spending-and-financing.

37   Avik Roy, "The Myth of Medicare's 'Low Administrative Costs,'" *Forbes*, June 30, 2011, https://www.forbes.com/sites/theapothecary/2011/06/30/the-myth-of-medicares-low-administrative-costs.

38   American Hospital Association, "New Report Shows Regulatory Burden Overwhelming Providers, Diverting Clinicians from Patient Care," press

release, October 25, 2017, https://www.aha.org/press-releases/2017-10-25-new-report-shows-regulatory-burden-overwhelming-providers-diverting.

39 Keith, "Unpacking the House Medicare-for-All Bill."

40 Brent Scher, "Jayapal Admits Her Medicare for All Bill Would Kill 1 Million Private Insurance Jobs," *Washington Free Beacon*, May 1, 2019, https://freebeacon.com/politics/jayapal-admits-her-medicare-for-all-bill-would-kill-one-million-private-insurance-jobs.

41 Keith, "Unpacking the House Medicare-for-All Bill."

42 "History," Centers for Medicare & Medicaid Services, modified August 5, 2019, https://www.cms.gov/About-CMS/Agency-information/History.

43 Avik Roy, "Saving Medicare from Itself," *National Affairs*, Summer 2011, https://www.nationalaffairs.com/publications/detail/saving-medicare-from-itself.

44 John Daniel Davidson, "50 Years Later, Medicaid and Medicare Still Spend Us into Oblivion," *The Federalist*, July 31, 2015, http://thefederalist.com/2015/07/31/medicare-medicaid-same-problems-50-years-ago.

45 1974 Annual Report of the Board of Trustees of the Federal Supplementary Medical Insurance Trust Fund, June 3, 1974. Centers for Medicare & Medicaid Services, https://www.cms.gov/Research-Statistics-Data-and-Systems/Statistics-Trends-and-Reports/ReportsTrustFunds/Downloads/TR1974SMI.zip, table B-12.

46 Allen R. Nissenson and Richard A. Rettig, "Medicare's End-Stage Renal Disease Program: Current Status and Future Prospects," *Health Affairs*, January/February 1999, https://www.healthaffairs.org/doi/pdf/10.1377/hlthaff.18.1.161, exhibit 2.

47 "Are Health Care Reform Cost Estimates Reliable?," Joint Economic Committee, July 31, 2009, https://www.jec.senate.gov/public/_cache/files/5802c84c-e821-4ab3-baeb-793f3ae2e036/are-health-care-reform-cost-estimates-reliable-july-31-2009.pdf.

48 Roy, "Saving Medicare from Itself."

49 Boards of Trustees, Federal Hospital Insurance and Federal Supplementary Medical Insurance Trust Funds, "2019 Annual Report," Washington, D.C., April 22, 2019, https://www.cms.gov/Research-Statistics-Data-and-Systems/Statistics-Trends-and-Reports/ReportsTrustFunds/Downloads/TR2019.pdf.

50 Davidson, "50 Years."

51 Jed Graham, "ObamaCare Medicaid Costs Rocket 49% Above Estimates," *Investor's Business Daily*, July 21, 2016, https://www.investors.com/news/obamacare-medicaid-costs-rocket-49-past-estimates.

52 Tessa Stuart and Jann S. Wenner, "Nancy Pelosi: The Rolling Stone Interview," *Rolling Stone*, February 27, 2019, https://www.rollingstone.com/politics/politics-features/nancy-pelosi-trump-interview-797209.

53 Todd Spangler, "US Senator Debbie Stabenow Wants Medicare Buy-In for Folks 50 and Older," *Detroit Free Press*, February 13, 2019, https://www.freep.com/story/news/local/michigan/2019/02/13/debbie-stabenow-medicare-coverage-michigan/2860052002.

54 Medicare at 50 Act, S. 470, 116th Cong. (2019).

55 "Senator Stabenow Announces Medicare at 55 Act," Debbie Stabenow, United States Senator for Michigan, August 3, 2017, https://www.stabenow.senate.gov/news/senator-stabenow-announces-medicare-at-55-act.

56　"The Medicare for America Act of 2018," United States Representative Rosa DeLauro, accessed March 25, 2019, https://delauro.house.gov/sites/delauro.house.gov/files/Medicare_for_America_Summary.pdf.

57　"The Medicare for America Act of 2018."

58　Jonathan Cohn, "2 Liberal Democrats Are Promoting a Twist on 'Medicare for All,'" *Huffington Post*, February 17, 2019, https://www.huffpost.com/entry/deluaro-schakowsky-medicare-for-america-all_n_5c672cc6e4b05c889d1f4bc9.

59　"The Medicare for America Act of 2018."

60　"The Medicare for America Act of 2018."

61　"The Medicare for America Act of 2018."

62　Medicare-X Choice Act of 2019, S. 981, 116th Cong. (2019).

63　Medicare-X Choice Act of 2019, H.R. 2000, 116th Cong. (2019).

64　"The Medicare-X Choice Act of 2019," Michael Bennet, U.S. Senator for Colorado, accessed April 26, 2019, https://www.bennet.senate.gov/public/_cache/files/3/c/3c7d1c24-3993-4905-b25e-cc6b49bf198e/D805D5EEA2960A53F958348F15A847E6.medicare-x-2019-one-pager.pdf.

65　"The Medicare-X Choice Act of 2019."

66　Jeff Stein, "'Bring It On': Biden and Sanders Teams Kick Off Debate over Medicare-for-All," *Washington Post*, April 29, 2019, https://www.washingtonpost.com/us-policy/2019/04/29/bring-it-biden-sanders-teams-kick-off-debate-over-medicare-for-all.

67　Helen A. Halpin and Peter Harbage, "The Origins and Demise of the Public Option," *Health Affairs*, June 2010, https://www.healthaffairs.org/doi/full/10.1377/hlthaff.2010.0363.

68　Choose Medicare Act, S. 1261, 116th Cong. (2019).

69　Choose Medicare Act, H.R. 2463, 116th Cong. (2019).

70　Choose Medicare Act, H.R. 2463.

71　Choose Medicare Act, H.R. 2463.

72　Chris Murphy, "Senators Introduce 'Choose Medicare Act' to Make Medicare Available to Everyone," press release, May 1, 2019, https://www.feinstein.senate.gov/public/index.cfm/press-releases?ID=156BBAE3-3135-4FD4-9B6A-8955F8764B20.

73　Alice Miranda Ollstein and Adam Cancryn, "Democrats' Plan to Neuter Medicare for All Irks Liberals," *Politico*, January 22, 2019, https://www.politico.com/story/2019/01/22/democrats-medicare-for-all-obamacare-1094146.

74　"Schatz, Luján Reintroduce Legislation to Create Public Health Care Option," Brian Schatz, United States Senator for Hawai'i, February 14, 2019, https://www.schatz.senate.gov/press-releases/schatz-lujn-reintroduce-legislation-to-create-public-health-care-option.

75　"Schatz, Luján Reintroduce Legislation."

76　State Public Option Act, S. 489, 116th Cong. (2019).

77　CAP Health Policy Team, "Medicare Extra for All," *Center for American Progress*, February 22, 2018, https://www.americanprogress.org/issues/healthcare/reports/2018/02/22/447095/medicare-extra-for-all.

78　CAP Health Policy Team, "Medicare Extra for All."

79 CAP Health Policy Team, "Medicare Extra for All."

80 CAP Health Policy Team, "Medicare Extra for All."

81 CAP Health Policy Team, "Medicare Extra for All."

82 CAP Health Policy Team, "Medicare Extra for All."

83 Healthy California Act, SB-562, California Legislature (2017).

84 Mac Taylor and Michael Cohen, "Fiscal Impact Estimate Report, 17-0019," Legislative Analyst's Office, October 9, 2017, https://oag.ca.gov/system/files/initiatives/pdfs/fiscal-impact-estimate-report%2817-0019%29.pdf.

85 Rebecca C. Lewis, "No State Senate Single-Payer Vote Before 2020," City and State NY, April 25, 2019, https://www.cityandstateny.com/articles/policy/health-care/no-state-senate-single-payer-vote-2020.html.

86 RAND Corporation, "Single-Payer Health Plan in New York State Could Cover All without Increasing Total Health Spending if Cost Growth Slows," press release, August 1, 2018, https://www.rand.org/news/press/2018/08/01.html.

87 Rachel Silberstein, "Single-Payer Healthcare Campaign Kicks Off in Albany," *Times Union*, February 11, 2019, https://www.timesunion.com/news/article/Single-payer-campaign-kicks-off-in-Albany-13607676.php.

88 Jodi L. Liu, Chapin White, Sarah A. Nowak, Asa Wilks, Jamie Ryan, and Christine Eibner, *An Assessment of the New York Health Act: A Single-Payer Option for New York State* (Santa Monica, CA: RAND Corporation, 2018), p. 71.

89 Nick Niedzwiadek and Sally Goldenberg, "Labor Divided Over Albany's Ambitious Single-Payer Healthcare Bill," *Politico*, December 5, 2018, https://www.politico.com/states/new-york/albany/story/2018/12/04/labor-divided-over-albanys-ambitious-single-payer-health-care-bill-728332.

90 Rachel Silberstein, "Cuomo: Universal Healthcare Easier to Implement on Federal Level," *Times Union*, August 30, 2018, https://www.timesunion.com/news/article/Cuomo-Universal-healthcare-easier-on-federal-13194080.php.

91 Proposal for Affordable Health Coverage Option, HB19-1004, Colorado General Assembly, 1st Reg. Sess., 72nd Gen. Assembly (2019), https://leg.colorado.gov/bills/hb19-1004.

92 Associated Press, "Colorado Lawmakers Approve Bill to Develop State Insurance Option," *KDVR*, April 23, 2019, https://kdvr.com/2019/04/23/colorado-lawmakers-approve-bill-to-develop-state-insurance-option.

93 Joseph O'Sullivan, "Washingtonians to Get Public Option on State's Health-Insurance Exchange," *Seattle Times*, May 13, 2019, https://www.seattletimes.com/seattle-news/politics/inslee-signs-bill-creating-a-public-option-for-washingtons-health-insurance-exchange.

94 "Public Opinion on Single-Payer."

95 "Public Opinion on Single-Payer."

96 Ashley Kirzinger, Cailey Muñana, Lunna Lopes, Liz Hamel, and Mollyann Brodie, "KFF Health Tracking Poll—June 2019: Health Care in the Democratic Primary and Medicare-for-All," Kaiser Family Foundation, June 18, 2019, https://www.kff.org/health-reform/poll-finding/kff-health-tracking-poll-june-2019.

97 "Public Opinion on Single-Payer."

CHAPTER THREE: THE MARCH TO A SINGLE-PAYER PLAN

1   Lorne Brown and Doug Taylor, "The Birth of Medicare," *Canadian Dimension*, July 3, 2012, https://canadiandimension.com/articles/view/the-birth-of-medicare.

2   "Co-operative Commonwealth Federation," CBC, accessed March 28, 2019, https://www.cbc.ca/history/EPISCONTENTSE1EP13CH3PA1LE.html; Neil Babaluk, "History Idol: Tommy Douglas," Canada's History, March 10, 2010, https://www.canadashistory.ca/explore/politics-law/history-idol-tommy-douglas.

3   Brown and Taylor, "The Birth."

4   "The Fight for Medicare," CBC, accessed March 28, 2019, https://www.cbc.ca/history/EPISCONTENTSE1EP15CH2PA4LE.html.

5   "The Fight for Medicare."

6   "The Fight for Medicare."

7   Brown and Taylor, "The Birth."

8   Brown and Taylor, "The Birth"; David Hutton, "Judge Emmett Hall's Work Paved the Way for Medicare," *Saskatoon StarPhoenix*, January 9, 2017, https://thestarphoenix.com/news/saskatchewan/canada-150-father-of-medicare-hall-among-provinces-greatest-assets.

9   Brown and Taylor, "The Birth."

10 Canada Health Act, R.S.C. 1985, c. C-6, §§ 8–12.

11 Canada Health Act.

12 Katherine Ward, "Few Canadians Have Early Access to Home Palliative Care: Study," *Global News*, September 19, 2018, https://globalnews.ca/news/4466707/palliative-care-study-canada.

13 Ward, "Few Canadians."

14 Anya Humphrey, "Grieving in Colour—Part I," *Conversations on Dying*, January 25, 2016, http://conversationsondying.com/2016/01/25/grieving-in-colour.

15 Humphrey, "Grieving."

16 "Get Medical Advice: Telehealth Ontario," Ontario.ca, accessed March 12, 2019, https://www.ontario.ca/page/get-medical-advice-telehealth-ontario; Humphrey, "Grieving."

17 Ward, "Few Canadians."

18 Humphrey, "Grieving."

19 Ward, "Few Canadians."

20 "Palliative Care in Canada Inconsistent, Patients Say," Canadian Institute for Health Information, September 2018, https://www.cihi.ca/en/access-data-and-reports/access-to-palliative-care-in-canada/palliative-care-in-canada-inconsistent-patients-say.

21 Canadian Institute for Health Information, *Access to Palliative Care in Canada* (Ottawa, ON: CIHI, 2018), https://www.cihi.ca/sites/default/files/document/access-palliative-care-2018-en-web.pdf.

22 "Palliative Care in Canada Inconsistent."

23 Aaron Derfel, "Quebec's Surgical Wait-Times Warrior Now in Fight Over His Wife's Care," *Montreal Gazette*, August 8, 2018, https://montrealgazette.com/news/local-news/quebecs-surgical-wait-times-warrior-now-in-fight-over-his-wifes-care.

24 John J. Morris, Lawrence M. Kwinter, Jacques Gauthier, Fay K. Brunning,

Michael K. McKelvey, Anne C. Corbett, and Larry R. Jackie, "Canada: The Impact of the Supreme Court of Canada's Decision in Chaoulli vs. Quebec (Attorney General)," *Mondaq*, September 27, 2005, http://www.mondaq.com/article.asp?article_id=34952&signup=true.

25 Morris et al., "Impact."

26 Chaoulli v. Quebec (Attorney General), 2005 SCC 35, [2005] 1 S.C.R. 791 (CanLII).

27 Sierra Dean, "Canada's Landmark Chaoulli Decision: A Vital Blueprint for Change in the Canadian Health Care System," *Law and Business Review of the Americas* 13, no. 2 (2007): 417–450.

28 Chaoulli v. Quebec.

29 Andrew Street, "Britain's National Health Service: One Model, Four Systems," *The Conversation*, September 25, 2017, https://theconversation.com/britains-national-health-service-one-model-four-systems-81579; "Why Do We Pay National Insurance?" BBC News, April 8, 2010, http://www.bbc.co.uk/newsbeat/article/10078062/why-do-we-pay-national-insurance.

30 James Connington, "What Conditions and Treatments Aren't Covered on the NHS—and How Much Do They Cost?," *The Telegraph*, May 25, 2018, https://www.telegraph.co.uk/money/consumer-affairs/conditions-treatments-arent-covered-nhs-much-do-cost; "NHS Prescription Charges," Politics.co.uk, accessed March 28, 2019, https://www.politics.co.uk/reference/nhs-prescription-charges.

31 Peter Greengross, Ken Grant, and Elizabeth Collini, "The History and Development of the UK National Health Service 1948–1999," 2nd ed., DFID Health Systems Resource Center, July 1999, https://assets.publishing.service.gov.uk/media/57a08d91e5274a31e000192c/The-history-and-development-of-the-UK-NHS.pdf.

32 Health Foundation, "The Emergency Hospital Service (Later Emergency Medical Service) Was Established in 1939," Policy Navigator, https://navigator.health.org.uk/content/emergency-hospital-service-later-emergency-medical-service-was-established-1939-1.

33 Denis Campbell, "Nye Bevan's Dream: A History of the NHS," *The Guardian*, January 18, 2016, https://www.theguardian.com/society/2016/jan/18/nye-bevan-history-of-nhs-national-health-service.

34 Health Foundation, "The Emergency Hospital Service."

35 Sir William Beveridge, "Social Insurance and Allied Services," originally published 1942, BBC News, http://news.bbc.co.uk/2/shared/bsp/hi/pdfs/19_07_05_beveridge.pdf, p. 11.

36 "Fact File: Beveridge Report," BBC, 2005, http://www.bbc.co.uk/history/ww2peopleswar/timeline/factfiles/nonflash/a1143578.shtml.

37 Ronan Burtenshaw, "Summoning the Future," *Jacobin*, February 2018, https://jacobinmag.com/2018/02/summoning-the-future.

38 Campbell, "Bevan's Dream."

39 Greengross, Grant, and Collini, "The History and Development of the UK National Health Service," p. 6

40 Campbell, "Bevan's Dream."

41 Rachel Thompson, "'Not Thin Enough': The People with Anorexia Being Refused Treatment," *Mashable*, March 1, 2019, https://mashable.com/article/dump-the-scales-eating-disorder-campaign; Michael Yong, "Bristol Woman

Opens Up About Being Groomed and Abused by Man from Church," *Bristol Live*, July 13, 2018, https://www.bristolpost.co.uk/news/bristol-news/being-abused-12-man-church-1780576.

42 Mark Smith, "My Heart Nearly Stopped After Hiding My Anorexia from My Family for Four Years," *Wales Online*, February 6, 2019, https://www.walesonline.co.uk/news/health/my-heart-nearly-stopped-after-15787929.

43 Smith, "My Heart."

44 Smith, "My Heart."

45 Tamara Berends, Berno van Meijel, Willem Nugteren, Mathijs Deen, Unna N. Danner, Hans W. Hoek, and Annemarie A. van Elburg, "Rate, Timing and Predictors of Relapse in Patients with Anorexia Nervosa Following a Relapse Prevention Program: A Cohort Study," *BMC Psychiatry* 16, no. 1 (2016): 316, https://dx.doi.org/10.1186%2Fs12888-016-1019-y.

46 Thompson, "Not Thin Enough."

47 Thompson, "Not Thin Enough."

48 Thompson, "Not Thin Enough."

49 Thompson, "Not Thin Enough."

50 "Resource Impact Report: Eating Disorders; Recognition and Treatment," NICE, May 2017, https://www.nice.org.uk/guidance/ng69/resources/resource-impact-report-pdf-4479687469.

51 Thompson, "Not Thin Enough."

52 Thompson, "Not Thin Enough."

53 "Resource Impact Report: Eating Disorders," section 1.2.

54 Hope Virgo, "Eating Disorders Are Not Just About Weight: #dumpthescales," Change.org, July 9, 2018, https://www.change.org/p/eating-disorders-are-not-just-about-weight-dumpthescales, "Petition Update: An Amazing First 24 Hours," https://www.change.org/p/eating-disorders-are-not-just-about-weight-dumpthescales/u/22992742.

55 Virgo, "Eating Disorders."

56 Azana Francis, "Women Told They Aren't Thin Enough for Eating Disorder Treatment, MP's Told," BBC News, October 16, 2018, https://www.bbc.com/news/uk-politics-45881914; Virgo, "Eating Disorders," "Petition Update: A Letter from Downing Street," https://www.change.org/p/eating-disorders-are-not-just-about-weight-dumpthescales/u/23755249.

57 "Who We Are," NICE: National Institute for Health and Care Excellence," accessed March 28, 2019, https://www.nice.org.uk/about/who-we-are.

CHAPTER FOUR: THE HORRORS OF SINGLE-PAYER INSURANCE—WAITS

1 Bacchus Barua and David Jacques, *Waiting Your Turn: Wait Times for Health Care in Canada* (Vancouver, BC: Fraser Institute, 2018), https://www.fraserinstitute.org/sites/default/files/waiting-your-turn-2018.pdf, p. iii.

2 Barua and Jacques, *Waiting Your Turn*, p. 1.

3 Barua and Jacques, *Waiting Your Turn*, p. 2.

4 Barua and Jacques, *Waiting Your Turn*, p. 2 (28.5 first segment + 16.6 second segment = 45.1 weeks total).

5 Barua and Jacques, *Waiting Your Turn*, p. 2 (17.5 +16.9 = 34.4).

6 Barua and Jacques, *Waiting Your Turn*, p. 6.

7 Barua and Jacques, *Waiting Your Turn*, p. 5.

8   Jackie Dunham, "Canadians Waiting Longer for Hip, Knee Replacements, and Cataract Surgeries: CIHI," CTV News, March 28, 2019, https://www.ctvnews.ca/health/canadians-waiting-longer-for-hip-knee-replacements-and-cataract-surgeries-cihi-1.4355589.

9   "Access to Health Care a Significant Problem for One-in-Five Canadians 55 and Older," Angus Reid Institute, August 7, 2019, http://angusreid.org/senior-health-access.

10 Colin Craig, "Healthcare Waiting Lists Unnecessarily Long," *Toronto Sun*, February 25, 2019, https://torontosun.com/opinion/columnists/craig-health-care-waiting-lists-unnecessarily-long.

11 Barua and Jacques, *Waiting Your Turn*, p. 10.

12 U.S. population = 327.2 million x 0.03 = 9,816,000.

13 "2nd Patient Dies After Being Sent Home from Abbotsford Regional Hospital," CBC News, February 24, 2017, https://www.cbc.ca/news/canada/british-columbia/abbotsford-regional-hospital-mary-louise-murphy-1.3998729.

14 "2nd Patient Dies."

15 Michael Tutton, "The Awful Death of Jack Webb: Wife Tells How Crowded Hospital Failed Her Husband," CTV News, April 25, 2017, https://www.ctvnews.ca/health/the-awful-death-of-jack-webb-wife-tells-how-crowded-hospital-failed-her-husband-1.3383952.

16 Tutton, "Jack Webb."

17 Tutton, "Jack Webb."

18 Tutton, "Jack Webb."

19 Tutton, "Jack Webb."

20 Michael Tutton, "Halifax Hospital Rewrites Wait-time Rules After Man's Wretched Death," CTV News, October 9, 2017, https://www.ctvnews.ca/health/halifax-hospital-rewrites-wait-time-rules-after-man-s-wretched-death-1.3625051.

21 "Boy, 3, Died 'Waiting to See Doctor' at Birmingham Hospital," BBC News, November 21, 2017, https://www.bbc.com/news/uk-england-birmingham-42072279.

22 Alex Matthews, "Three-Year-Old Boy Died in His Father's Arms in Children's Hospital A&E After He Was Kept Waiting for More Than an Hour," *Daily Mail*, November 22, 2017, https://www.dailymail.co.uk/news/article-5107493/Boy-died-father-s-arms-children-s-hospital-E.html.

23 Matthews, "Three-Year-Old Boy."

24 Vik Adhopia, "Canadian's Healthcare 'One Issue per Visit' Problem," CBC News, March 20, 2019, https://www.cbc.ca/news/health/second-opinion-one-problem-visit-1.5061506.

25 "Doctors (Indicator)," OECD, 2019, https://data.oecd.org/healthres/doctors.htm; "Hospital Beds," OECD, 2019, https://data.oecd.org/healtheqt/hospital-beds.htm#indicator-chart.

26 Glen Whiffen and Nancy King, "Atlantic Canada Needs More Doctors: Where Are They?" *Chronicle Herald*, January 25, 2019, https://www.thechronicleherald.ca/in-depth/doctor-shortage/atlantic-canada-needs-more-doctors-where-are-they-278198.

27 Max Winkelman, "Addressing a Nursing Shortage," *BC Local News*, March 21, 2019, https://www.bclocalnews.com/opinion/addressing-a-nursing-shortage.

28 Stephanie Marin, "One in Five Newly Certified Medical Specialists Unemployed in 2017, Study Shows," CTV News, May 1, 2019, https://www.ctvnews.ca/health/one-in-five-newly-certified-medical-specialists-unemployed-in-2017-study-shows-1.4403295.

29 Kelly Grant, "Nearly One in Five New Specialists Doctors Can't Find a Job After Certification, Survey Shows," *Globe and Mail*, May 1, 2019, https://www.theglobeandmail.com/canada/article-nearly-one-in-five-new-specialist-doctors-cant-find-a-job-after.

30 "Our History," Cambie Surgery Centre, https://www.cambiesurgery.com/about-us.

31 Doug Ward, "A New Day for Healthcare," *Vancouver Sun*, April 8, 2002, https://www.brianday.ca/news/a-new-day-for-health-care.

32 Ian Mulgrew, "Ottawa's Response to Medicare Challenge Is, Be Afraid," *Vancouver Sun*, April 18, 2019, https://vancouversun.com/news/national/ian-mulgrew-ottawas-response-to-medicare-challenge-is-be-afraid.

33 Pamela Fayerman, "Medicine Matters: The Cosmetic Roots of Private Surgery Clinics in BC," *Vancouver Sun*, April 24, 2017, https://vancouversun.com/news/staff-blogs/medicine-matters-the-cosmetic-roots-of-private-surgery-clinics-in-bc; Ian Mulgrew, "Dr. Brian Day Takes the Stand in Court, Has His Say on Access to Private Healthcare," *Vancouver Sun*, September 19, 2018, https://vancouversun.com/news/local-news/ian-mulgrew-dr-brian-day-takes-the-stand-in-court-has-his-say-on-access-to-private-health-care.

34 Martha Dillman, "Sudbury Patient Shares Experience of Being Placed in a Hospital Bathroom for Care," CBC News, February 26, 2018, https://www.cbc.ca/news/canada/sudbury/sudbury-hospital-patient-bathroom-1.4549296.

35 Dillman, "Sudbury Patient."

36 Trevor Dunn, "Bleeding Internally, 'Screaming in Pain' Brampton Woman Spent 5 Days in Hospital Hallway," CBC News, April 13, 2017, https://www.cbc.ca/news/canada/toronto/brampton-woman-hospital-hallway-1.4070379.

37 Dunn, "Bleeding Internally."

38 Alison Motluk, "Hallway Healthcare," *Toronto Life*, April 16, 2018, https://torontolife.com/city/woman-waited-47-hours-surgery-broken-bones-cracked-ribs-internal-bleeding.

39 Motluk, "Hallway Healthcare."

40 Motluk, "Hallway Healthcare."

41 Ryan W. Morasiewicz and Shahdin Farsai, "Case Brief: Cambie Surgeries Corp. V. Medical Services Commission of British Columbia—Chaoulli Revisited," Miller Thomson, November 21, 2016, https://www.millerthomson.com/en/publications/communiques-and-updates/health-communique/november-21-2016-health/case-brief-cambie-surgeries-corp-v-medical-services-commission-of-british-columbia-chaoulli-revisited.

42 Ian Mulgrew, "Medicare Expert, Lawyer Spar to End Landmark Trial," *Vancouver Sun*, July 18, 2019, https://vancouversun.com/opinion/columnists/medicare-trial-evidence-comes-to-an-end.

43 Colin Craig, "Policy Brief: The Flight of the Sick," Second Street, March 2019, https://www.secondstreet.org/wp-content/uploads/2019/04/Policy-Brief-Flight-of-the-Sick.pdf.

44 Jane Stevenson, "More Canadians Leaving Country for Healthcare: Report,"

Toronto Sun, March 12, 2019, https://torontosun.com/news/national/canadians-continue-to-leave-the-country-for-health-care-says-new-report.

45 Chris Kitching and Alison Stacey, "Nurse 'Not Sick Enough' for NHS Treatment Pays £42k for Transplant in Mexico," *Mirror*, March 4, 2019, https://www.mirror.co.uk/news/uk-news/nurse-not-sick-enough-nhs-14085001; Alison Stacey, "NHS Nurse Told 'Not Ill Enough' for Treatment Flies to Mexico for Life Saving Care," *Birmingham Mail*, March 4, 2019, https://www.birminghammail.co.uk/black-country/nhs-15911741.

46 Kitching and Stacey, "Nurse 'Not Sick Enough.'"

47 "HSCT," MS Society, accessed March 13, 2019, https://www.mssociety.org.uk/about-ms/treatments-and-therapies/disease-modifying-therapies/hsct.

48 Kitching and Stacey, "Nurse 'Not Sick Enough.'"

49 Kitching and Stacey, "Nurse 'Not Sick Enough.'"

50 Michele Sponagle, "Surgery in Paradise: Canadians Explore Cayman Islands for Destination Healthcare," YouAreUNLTD, February 20, 2019, https://www.youareunltd.com/2019/02/20/surgery-in-paradise-canadians-explore-cayman-islands-for-destination-healthcare.

51 "Medical Tourism Growing in Popularity with Canadians," CTV News, September 12, 2016, https://www.ctvnews.ca/health/health-headlines/medical-tourism-growing-in-popularity-with-canadians-1.3069445.

52 Fiona Tapp, "Why Canadians Are Increasingly Seeking Medical Treatment Abroad," Yahoo! News, June 29, 2017, https://news.yahoo.com/why-canadians-increasingly-seeking-medical-080830117.html.

53 Tapp, "Why Canadians."

54 Carl Baker, "NHS Key Statistics: England, May 2019," U.K. Commons Briefing papers CBP-7281, May 30, 2019, https://researchbriefings.parliament.uk/ResearchBriefing/Summary/CBP-7281, p. 11.

55 Susannah Thraves, "My Wait for NHS Surgery Has Caused Me Further Pain," *The Guardian*, August 7, 2019, https://www.theguardian.com/commentisfree/2019/aug/07/wait-nhs-surgery-pain-patients-england-distress.

56 Thraves, "My Wait."

57 "Guide to NHS Waiting Times in England," NHS, November 14, 2016, https://www.nhs.uk/using-the-nhs/nhs-services/hospitals/guide-to-nhs-waiting-times-in-england.

58 Baker, "NHS Key Statistics," p. 13.

59 "'Worthless' NHS Treatment Time Guarantee Broken 200 Times a Day, Lib Dems Say," *Daily Gazette*, February 26, 2019, https://www.gazette-news.co.uk/news/national/17459869.worthless-nhs-treatment-time-guarantee-broken-200-times-a-day-lib-dems-say.

60 Baker, "NHS Key Statistics," p. 13.

61 Commons Select Committee, "NHS Failure to Meet Waiting Times Targets Risks Patients' Lives," U.K. Government, June 12, 2019, https://www.parliament.uk/business/committees/committees-a-z/commons-select/public-accounts-committee/news-parliament-2017/nhs-waiting-times-report-published-17-19.

62 Commons Select Committee, "NHS Failure."

63 Alex Matthews-King, "Cancer Treatment Waiting Times See 'Concerning

Spike' as NHS Plans to Ditch Key Measures," *Independent*, March 14, 2019, https://www.independent.co.uk/news/health/nhs-cancer-waiting-time-ae-surgery-official-figures-a8822656.html.

64   "Ellie-May Clark Died After Potentially Life-Saving Treatment Missed," BBC News, February 26, 2018, https://www.bbc.com/news/uk-wales-north-west-wales-43196732.

65   "Five-Year-Old Girl Died After GP Turned Her Away for Being Five Minutes Late for Appointment, Inquest Hears," *The Telegraph*, February 26, 2018, https://www.telegraph.co.uk/news/2018/02/26/five-year-old-girl-died-gp-turned-away-five-minutes-late-appointment.

66   "Ellie-May Clark Died."

67   "Ellie-May Clark Died"; Chris Perez, "Girl Died Hours After Doctor Turned Her Away for Being a Few Minutes Late," *New York Post*, February 26, 2018, https://nypost.com/2018/02/26/girl-dies-hours-after-doctor-turned-her-away-for-being-a-few-minutes-late.

68   "Ellie-May Clark Died."

69   "Ellie-May Clark Died."

70   "Five-Year-Old Girl Died."

71   "Five-Year-Old Girl Died."

72   "Ellie-May Clark Died."

73   "Five-Year-Old Girl Died."

74   "Five-Year-Old Girl Died."

75   "Ellie-May Clark Died."

76   "Ellie-May Clark Died."

77   "Girl, 5, Died After Doctor Turned Her Away for Being 10 Minutes Late," Sky News, February 27, 2018, https://news.sky.com/story/girl-5-died-after-doctor-turned-her-away-for-being-10-minutes-late-11269249.

78   "Regulation 28: Report to Prevent Future Deaths," Courts and Tribunals Judiciary, accessed September 20, 2019, https://www.judiciary.uk/wp-content/uploads/2018/06/Ellie-Clark-2018-0066_Redacted.pdf.

79   "Ellie-May Clark Died."

80   Nick McDermott, "War of Wards: NHS Beds Crisis 'Critical' as More Sick Brits Left Stranded in Hospital Corridors Last Month Than at the Height of Winter," *The Sun*, June 22, 2019, https://www.thesun.co.uk/news/9349854/nhs-beds-crisis-patients-hospital-corridors-summer.

81   McDermott, "War of Wards."

82   Nick Triggle, "NHS Signals Four-Hour A&E Target May End," BBC News, March 11, 2019, https://www.bbc.com/news/health-47485592.

83   Baker, "NHS Key Statistics," p. 4.

84   Baker, "NHS Key Statistics," p. 3.

85   Haroon Siddique, "Record Number of NHS A&E Patients Wait Over Four Hours on Trolleys," *The Guardian*, August 8, 2019, https://www.theguardian.com/society/2019/aug/08/millions-waiting-for-nhs-operations-in-england-the-highest-total-on-record.

86   Nick Triggle, "A&E Waits at Worst Level for 15 Years in England," BBC News, February 14, 2019, https://www.bbc.com/news/health-47229719.

87   Nick McDermott, "NHS Waits Warning: Millions of Sick Brits May Face Longer Delays for Emergency Treatment as NHS Bids to Axe Four-Hour

Target," *The Sun*, January 29, 2019, https://www.thesun.co.uk/news/8302068/four-hour-waiting-time-ae.

88 Baker, "NHS Key Statistics," p. 8.
89 Carl Baker, "NHS Winter Pressures in England, 2017/18," U.K. Commons Briefing papers CBP-8210, April 4, 2018, https://researchbriefings.parliament.uk/ResearchBriefing/Summary/CBP-8210#fullreport, p. 4.
90 Baker, "NHS Winter Pressures," p. 7.
91 Baker, "NHS Winter Pressures," p. 13.
92 Harriet Agerholm, "Ambulances Filmed Queuing Outside Essex Hospital A&E as NHS Crisis Deepens," *Independent*, January 5, 2018, https://www.independent.co.uk/news/health/nhs-winter-crisis-ambulances-video-chelmsford-hospital-accident-emergency-patients-beds-space-staff-a8144146.html.
93 Baker, "NHS Winter Pressures," p. 8.
94 Baker, "NHS Winter Pressures," p. 9.
95 Denis Campbell, "16,900 People in a Week Kept in NHS Ambulances Waiting for Hospital Care," *The Guardian*, January 4, 2018, https://www.theguardian.com/society/2018/jan/04/16900-people-in-a-week-kept-in-nhs-ambulances-waiting-for-hospital-care.
96 Matt Graveling, "Patient Waited 62 Hours for Ambulance," August 23, 2018, BBC News, https://www.bbc.com/news/uk-45246939.
97 Graveling, "Patient Waited 62 Hours."
98 Ben Glaze, "Tens of Thousands of Ambulance Staff Have Quit the NHS in Last Nine Years," *Mirror*, May 7, 2019, https://www.mirror.co.uk/news/politics/tens-thousands-ambulance-staff-quit-15005720.
99 Nicola Small, "NHS Spends £215,000 A DAY on Private Ambulances Because of Paramedic Shortage," *Mirror*, October 20, 2018, https://www.mirror.co.uk/news/uk-news/nhs-spends-215000-day-private-13449055.
100 Sarah Marsh, "Struggling Ambulance Trust Considers Using Volunteer and Military Drivers," *The Guardian*, August 2, 2018, https://www.theguardian.com/society/2018/aug/02/struggling-ambulance-trust-considers-using-volunteer-drivers.
101 Matt Bodell, "Half of NHS Staff Are Working Unpaid Overtime and the Majority Want to Leave Their Role," Nursing Notes, February 27, 2019, https://nursingnotes.co.uk/half-of-nhs-staff-are-working-extra-unpaid-hours-and-the-majority-want-to-leave-their-role.
102 Lucy Johnston, "One in Four NHS Nurses Takes Sick Days Due to Stress," *Mirror*, December 22, 2018, https://www.mirror.co.uk/news/uk-news/one-four-nhs-nurses-takes-13770027.
103 Zoe Drewett, "Why Have 160,000 Nurses Quit the NHS?," Metro, March 27, 2019, https://metro.co.uk/2019/03/27/160000-nurses-quit-nhs-9034145.
104 Anonymous, "My Job as a Doctor in Today's NHS Is Draining Me of Humanity," *The Guardian*, February 7, 2019, https://www.theguardian.com/society/2019/feb/07/job-doctor-todays-nhs-draining-humanity.
105 Irene Papanicolas, Liana R. Woskie, and Ashish Jha, "Health Care Spending in the United States and Other High-Income Countries," Commonwealth Fund, March 13, 2018, https://www.commonwealthfund.org/publications/journal-article/2018/mar/health-care-spending-united-states-and-other-high-income.

106 "Doctors (Indicator)"; "Nurses (Indicator)," OECD, 2019, https://data.oecd.org/healthres/nurses.htm#indicator-chart.

107 Anita Charlesworth and Paul Johnson, eds., *Securing the Future: Funding Health and Social Care to the 2030s* (London: Institute for Fiscal Studies, May 2018), https://www.ifs.org.uk/uploads/R143.pdf, p. 30.

108 NHS Improvement, *Performance of the NHS Provider Sector for the Quarter Ended 31 December 2018*, 2018, https://improvement.nhs.uk/documents/4942/Performance_of_the_NHS_provider_sector_for_the_quarter_ended_31_Dec_2018.pdf, p. 27 (these are the most recent numbers, released March 7, 2019).

109 Anna Smith, "NHS Employers Warning on Level of NHS Vacancies," PharmaTimes, January 25, 2019, http://www.pharmatimes.com/news/nhs_employers_responds_to_93,964_nhs_vacancies_1276216.

110 Hannah C.P. Wilson and Arabella L. Simpkin, "Why Are So Many Doctors Quitting the NHS?—It's Time to Ask the Right Questions," *BMJ Opinion*, January 25, 2019, https://blogs.bmj.com/bmj/2019/01/25/why-are-so-many-doctors-quitting-the-nhs-its-time-to-ask-the-right-questions.

111 Martin Bagot, "NHS Crisis Deepens as 40% of GPs Set to Quit over Next Five Years in Mass Exodus," *Mirror*, February 27, 2019, https://www.mirror.co.uk/news/uk-news/nhs-crisis-deepens-40-gps-14062708.

112 The Health Foundation, King's Fund, and Nuffield Trust, *Closing the Gap: Key Areas for Action on the Health and Care Workforce*, March 2019, https://www.nuffieldtrust.org.uk/files/2019-03/1553101044_heaj6918-workforce-briefing-190320-web.pdf.

113 The Health Foundation et al., *Closing the Gap*, p. 2.

114 The Health Foundation et al., *Closing the Gap*, p. 17.

115 Anviksha Patel, "NHS Recruits 120 Overseas Doctors Towards Target of 2,000," *Pulse*, June 28, 2019, http://www.pulsetoday.co.uk/news/all-news/nhs-recruits-120-overseas-doctors-towards-target-of-2000/20038966.article.

116 Henry Bodkin, "Hospital Bosses Told to Get on a Plane and Find More Foreign Nurses to Work in the NHS," *The Telegraph*, March 23, 2019, https://www.telegraph.co.uk/news/2019/03/23/hospital-bosses-told-get-plane-find-foreign-nurses-work-nhs.

117 Maggie Baska, "NHS Plans Global Recruitment Drive for Thousands of Nurses," *People Management*, May 7, 2019, https://www.peoplemanagement.co.uk/news/articles/nhs-plans-global-recruitment-drive-thousands-nurses.

118 Michael Savage, "Plans to Hire Thousands of Foreign Nurses for NHS Is Axed," *The Guardian*, June 2, 2019, https://www.theguardian.com/society/2019/jun/02/foreign-nurses-target-cut-from-nhs-staffing-plan.

119 Alex Matthews-King, "NHS to Bring in 22,000 Non-Medical Staff to Divert Patients from Seeing GPs," *Independent*, January 31, 2019, https://www.independent.co.uk/news/health/gp-appointments-nhs-nurse-physio-pharmacist-employ-staff-funding-a8755311.html.

120 Laura Donnelly, Patrick Scott, and Jessica Carpani, "Alarm Raised Over Tripling in Cancelled NHS Appointments," *The Telegraph*, April 26, 2019, https://www.telegraph.co.uk/news/2019/04/26/alarm-raised-tripling-cancelled-nhs-appointments.

121 Baker, "NHS Key Statistics," p. 16.

122 Baker, "NHS Key Statistics," p. 16.

123 Baker, "NHS Key Statistics," p. 16.

124 Patrick Collinson, "Private Health Insurance Sales Surge amid NHS Crisis," *The Guardian*, January 15, 2017, https://www.theguardian.com/business/2017/jan/16/private-medical-insurance-sales-surge-health-nhs.

125 Thorlby and Arora, "The English Health Care System."

126 Sam Blanchard, "NHS Could Pay for 250,000 Patients Waiting Too Long for Surgery to Receive Treatment At Private Hospitals Under New Rules," *Daily Mail*, March 22, 2019, https://www.dailymail.co.uk/health/article-6838929/NHS-pay-250-000-extra-patients-year-sent-private-hospitals.html.

127 Kate Pickles, "Almost 300,000 More NHS Operations Could Be Carried Out Every Year If Staff Planned to Leave Earlier and Schedules Were More Organised, Watchdog Finds," *Daily Mail*, February 3, 2019, https://www.dailymail.co.uk/health/article-6664211/Almost-300-000-NHS-operations-carried-year-organised.html.

128 Sophie Borland, "NHS Stroke Patients Could Have to Travel 45 Minutes to Their Nearest Hospital Under Plans to Close a Third of Specialist Units," *Daily Mail*, January 24, 2019, https://www.dailymail.co.uk/news/article-6630397/NHS-stroke-patients-travel-45-minutes-nearest-hospital.html.

129 Denis Campbell, "NHS England Restricts Patients' Access to Cataract Removal," *The Guardian*, March 19, 2019, https://www.theguardian.com/politics/2019/mar/20/nhs-england-restricts-patients-access-to-cataract-removal.

130 "NHS Dentist Search Man Pulls Out Own Tooth After 18-Month Wait," BBC News, January 29, 2019, https://www.bbc.com/news/uk-england-cornwall-47010049.

131 "Man Pulls Out Own Tooth."

132 "Man Pulls Out Own Tooth."

133 "Man Pulls Out Own Tooth."

134 Gayle McDonald, "Cornwall Patients Face 65 Mile Trip to See an NHS Dentist," *Cornwall Live*, March 19, 2019, https://www.cornwalllive.com/news/cornwall-news/cornwall-patients-face-65-mile-2661968.

135 McDonald, "Cornwall Patients."

136 Greg Irving, Ana Luisa Neves, Hajira Dambha-Miller, Ai Oishi, Hiroko Tagashira, Anistasiya Verho, and John Holden, "International Variations in Primary Care Physician Consultation Time: A Systematic Review of 67 Countries," *BMJ* 7, no. 10 (October 2017), http://dx.doi.org/10.1136/bmjopen-2017-017902.

137 Lucia Binding, "NHS to Roll Out GP Group Appointments for Up to 15 Patients," Sky News, October 6, 2018, https://news.sky.com/story/nhs-to-roll-out-gp-group-appointments-for-up-to-15-patients-11518901.

138 Laura Donnelly, "GPs to See Patients in Groups of 15," *The Telegraph*, October 5, 2018, https://www.telegraph.co.uk/news/2018/10/05/gps-see-patients-groups-15.

139 Donnelly, "GPs to See Patients."

CHAPTER FIVE: THE HORRORS OF SINGLE-PAYER INSURANCE—ACCESS
TO CUTTING-EDGE TREATMENTS AND TECHNOLOGIES

1　Rachel Ross, "What Are CT Scans and How Do They Work?" Live Science, November 14, 2018, https://www.livescience.com/64093-ct-scan.html.

2　"Health Care Resources: Medical Technology," OECD, 2019, https://stats. oecd.org/index.aspx?queryid=30184.

3　Catherine Bergeron, Richard Fleet, Fatoumata Korika Tounkara, Isabelle Lavallée-Bourget, and Catherine Turgeon-Pelchat, "Lack of CT Scanner in a Rural Emergency Department Increases Inter-facility Transfers: A Pilot Study," BMC Research Notes 10 (2017): 772, https://dx.doi.org/10.1186%2 Fs13104-017-3071-1.

4　"The Canadian Medical Imaging Inventory, 2017," CADTH, March 2018, https://cadth.ca/canadian-medical-imaging-inventory-2017.

5　Barua and Jacques, Waiting Your Turn.

6　"The Canadian Medical Imaging Inventory, 2017."

7　Angela Gemmill, "Windsor Doctor Clears Up Discrepancies in PET Scanner Debate," CBC News, March 7, 2018, https://www.cbc.ca/news/canada/ sudbury/pet-scanner-windsor-sudbury-1.4564710.

8　"The Canadian Medical Imaging Inventory, 2017."

9　"Magnetic Resonance Imaging (MRI) Units (Indicator)," OECD, 2019, https://data.oecd.org/healtheqt/magnetic-resonance-imaging-mri-units. htm#indicator-chart.

10　Barua and Jacques, Waiting Your Turn.

11　"The Canadian Medical Imaging Inventory, 2017."

12　Greg Sutherland, Nigel Russell, Robyn Gibbard, and Alexandru Dobrescu, "The Value of Radiology, Part II," Conference Board of Canada, June 2019, https://car.ca/wp-content/uploads/2019/07/value-of-radiology-part-2-en.pdf, p. 5.

13　"Radiotherapy Equipment (Indicator)," OECD, 2019, https://data.oecd.org/ healtheqt/radiotherapy-equipment.htm.

14　"Mammography Machines (Indicator)," OECD, 2019, https://data.oecd.org/ healtheqt/mammography-machines.htm.

15　"Drug Spending at a Glance," Canadian Institute for Health Information, 2018, https://www.cihi.ca/sites/default/files/document/nhex-drug-infosheet-2018-en-web.pdf.

16　Doug Badger, "Examination of International Drug Pricing Policies in Selected Countries Shows Prevalent Government Control over Pricing and Restrictions on Access," Galen Institute, March 2019, https://galen.org/assets/ Badger-Report-March-2019.pdf.

17　Badger, "Examination of International Drug Pricing Policies."

18　Badger, "Examination of International Drug Pricing Policies."

19　Patented Medicine Prices Review Board, "Regulatory Process," Government of Canada, last modified October 9, 2018, http://pmprb-cepmb.gc.ca/en/ regulating-prices/regulatory-process.

20　Nicole Ireland, "'Unprecedented' Drug Shortages Affecting Many Canadians, New Survey Suggests," CBC News, December 10, 2018, https://www. cbc.ca/news/health/canadian-pharmacists-association-drug-shortage-survey-1.4938557.

21　Kelly Crowe, "It's Not Just the EpiPen: Canada Has 25 New Drug Shortages

This Week Alone," CBC News, September 8, 2018, https://www.cbc.ca/news/ health/second-opinion-drug-shortages180908-1.4815355.

22 "Drug Shortages Homepage," Drug Shortages Canada, https://www. drugshortagescanada.ca.

23 "CPhA Drug Shortages: A Survey of 1,500 Canadian Residents," Abacus Data, November 2018, http://www.pharmacists.ca/cpha-ca/assets/File/cpha-on-the-issues/DrugShortages_AbacusSurvey_November2018.pdf, p. 6.

24 "CADTH Common Drug Review (CDR)," CADTH, https://www.cadth.ca/ about-cadth/what-we-do/products-services/cdr.

25 "Canadian Drug Expert Committee (CDEC)," CADTH, https://www.cadth. ca/collaboration-and-outreach/advisory-bodies/canadian-drug-expert-committee-cdec.

26 Victoria Coles, "Pitfalls in Canada's Approach to Orphan Drugs," *Rare Disease Review*, November 23, 2017, https://www.rarediseasereview.org/ publications/2017/11/23/pitfalls-in-canadas-approach-to-orphan-drugs.

27 Coles, "Pitfalls."

28 Rosa Marchitelli, "Brothers Have the Same Deadly Disease but Only 1 Gets What Their Parents Hope Is Life-Saving Treatment," CBC News, May 5, 2019, https://www.cbc.ca/news/health/boy-with-cystic-fibrosis-denied-lifesaving-drug-1.5117469.

29 Marchitelli, "Brothers."

30 Carolyn Ray, "They Face Financial Ruin to Get a New Lung: Some Are Choosing to Die Instead," CBC News, March 13, 2019, https://www.cbc. ca/news/canada/nova-scotia/lung-transplants-atlantic-canada-toronto-financial-cost-1.5047818.

31 Diana Zlomislic, "Grief for Sharon Shamblaw, for Whom Ontario's Healthcare System Moved Too Slowly," *Star Edition*, May 15, 2016, https:// www.thestar.com/news/canada/2016/05/15/grief-for-sharon-shamblaw-for-whom-ontarios-health-care-system-moved-too-slowly.html.

32 Diana Zlomislic, "Sharon's Story: Trip to Buffalo for Stem-Cell Transplant Came Too Late," *The Star*, April 27, 2016, https://www.thestar.com/news/ gta/2016/04/27/sharons-story-trip-to-buffalo-for-stem-cell-transplant-came-too-late.html.

33 Zlomislic, "Grief."

34 Zlomislic, "Sharon's Story."

35 Zlomislic, "Grief."

36 Diane Zlomislic, "Ontario to Spend $100M Outsourcing Life-Saving Transplants to U.S.," *The Star*, April 19, 2016, https://www.thestar.com/ news/canada/2016/04/19/ontario-to-spend-100m-outsourcing-life-saving-transplants-to-us.html.

37 Zlomislic, "Ontario."

38 Zlomislic, "Ontario."

39 Zlomislic, "Sharon's Story."

40 Zlomislic, "Grief."

41 Zlomislic, "Sharon's Story."

42 Zlomislic, "Grief."

43 Zlomislic, "Grief."

44 Zlomislic, "Sharon's Story."

45 Zlomislic, "Grief."

46   J.C. Herbert Emery and Ronald Kneebone, "The Challenge of Defining Medicare Coverage in Canada," University of Calgary, School of Public Policy, SPP Research Papers 6, no. 32 (October 2013), https://www.policyschool.ca/wp-content/uploads/2016/03/emery-kneebone-medicare.pdf; p.1

47   Megan Griffith-Greene, "5 Medical Costs You May Have to Pay For," CBC News, February 5, 2015, https://www.cbc.ca/news/health/5-medical-costs-you-may-have-to-pay-for-1.2945539.

48   "Martin Agrees to Pharmacare Working Group," CBC News, September 14, 2004, https://www.cbc.ca/news/canada/martin-agrees-to-pharmacare-working-group-1.484770; Mark Kennedy, "Canada Is Years Behind on Healthcare Reform Due to Tory Lack of Action: Paul Martin," *National Post*, December 19, 2011, https://nationalpost.com/news/canada/canada-is-years-behind-on-health-care-reform-due-to-tory-lack-of-action-paul-martin.

49   David Ljunggren and Anna Mehler Paperny, "Exclusive: Canada Budget to Include Limited Coverage for Prescription Drugs—Sources," Reuters, January 31, 2019, https://ca.reuters.com/article/topNews/idCAKCN1PP2TL-OCATP.

50   "Moving Forward on Implementing National Pharmacare," Government of Canada, March 19, 2019, https://www.budget.gc.ca/2019/docs/themes/pharmacare-assurance-medicaments-en.html.

51   "Health Care Resources: Medical Technology," OECD, 2019, https://stats.oecd.org/index.aspx?queryid=30184.

52   "Health Care Resources: Medical Technology," see chart: "Mammographs total"; "Mammography Machines," OECD, 2019, https://data.oecd.org/healtheqt/mammography-machines.htm.

53   "Magnetic Resonance Imaging (MRI) Units (Indicator)."

54   Alex Matthews-King, "NHS Scanner and Radiologists Shortages Contributing to Thousands of Avoidable Heart Attack Deaths, Experts Warn," *Independent*, November 9, 2018, https://www.independent.co.uk/news/health/heart-attack-deaths-mri-nhs-scanner-radiologist-shortages-budget-a8622461.html.

55   "Medulloblastoma/PNET," Royal Marsden NHS Foundation Trust, https://www.royalmarsden.nhs.uk/your-care/cancer-types/paediatric-cancers/medulloblastomapnet.

56   "Medulloblastoma," National Cancer Institute Dictionary of Cancer Terms, https://www.cancer.gov/publications/dictionaries/cancer-terms/def/medulloblastoma.

57   "Medulloblastoma," St. Jude Children's Research Hospital, https://www.stjude.org/disease/medulloblastoma.html.

58   "Brain Tumour Boy Ashya King Back Home in Portsmouth," BBC News, July 3, 2015, https://www.bbc.com/news/uk-england-hampshire-33376284.

59   "Brain Tumour Boy Ashya King Is Free of Cancer After Proton Therapy, Parents Say," *The Telegraph*, March 23, 2015, https://www.telegraph.co.uk/news/health/children/11489212/Brain-tumour-boy-Ashya-King-is-free-of-cancer-parents-say.html.

60   Anthony Joseph, "I Want to Be a Chef When I'm Older: Ashya King Speaks for First Time Since Doctors Said His Cancer Is Unlikely to Return Three-and-a-Half Years After He Underwent Proton-Beam Therapy Abroad," *Daily Mail*, March 16, 2018, https://www.dailymail.co.uk/news/article-5508937/Ashya-King-reveals-wants-chef-beating-cancer.html.

61 "Proton Beam Therapy Program," Mayo Clinic, https://www.mayoclinic.org/
    departments-centers/proton-beam-therapy-program/sections/overview/ovc-
    20185491.

62 "Timeline: Proton Therapy," ProCure Proton Therapy Center, https://www.
    procure.com/Media/Fact-Sheets/Corporate/Proton-Therapy-Timeline.

63 Nicola Harley, "UK to Get First Proton Therapy Centre After Ashya King's
    Plight Raised Awareness of Vital Cancer Treatment," *The Telegraph*, May 20,
    2017, https://www.telegraph.co.uk/news/2017/05/20/uk-get-first-proton-
    therapy-centre-ashya-kings-plight-raised.

64 "Ashya King: NHS to Fund Prague Proton Beam Therapy," BBC News,
    September 26, 2014, https://www.bbc.com/news/uk-england-29386974.

65 "Ashya King Is Free of Cancer."

66 "NHS to Fund Prague Proton Beam Therapy."

67 Nadia Khomami and Jamie Doward, "Parents Arrested as Missing Ashya
    King Found by Police in Spain," *The Guardian*, August 30, 2014, https://www.
    theguardian.com/society/2014/aug/31/ashya-king-found-spain-parents-
    arrested.

68 Caroline Davies, "Ashya King Case: Timeline," *The Guardian*, September
    1, 2014, https://www.theguardian.com/society/2014/sep/01/ashya-king-
    timeline.

69 Joseph, "I Want to Be a Chef."

70 Joseph, "I Want to Be a Chef"; Gregory Walton, "Ashya King: Brain Tumour
    Boy Arrives in Prague for Proton Therapy," *The Telegraph*, September 16,
    2014, https://www.telegraph.co.uk/news/uknews/11096251/Ashya-King-
    brain-tumour-boy-arrives-in-Prague-for-proton-therapy.html.

71 Walton, "Brain Tumour Boy Arrives in Prague."

72 Joel Adams, "Ashya King Cleared of Cancer Three Years After His Parents
    Abducted Him from Hospital for Treatment Abroad," *The Telegraph*, March
    3, 2018, https://www.telegraph.co.uk/news/2018/03/03/ashya-king-cleared-
    cancer-three-years-parents-abducted-hospital.

73 Jane Dalton, "NHS 'Doesn't Have Enough Scanners' to Roll Out New Hi-Tech
    Method of Detecting Prostate Cancer," *Independent*, December 12, 2018,
    https://www.independent.co.uk/news/uk/home-news/prostate-cancer-nhs-
    scan-mri-treatment-biopsy-diagnosis-a8678501.html.

74 Dalton, "NHS 'Doesn't Have Enough Scanners.'"

75 Denis Campbell, "Hospitals Struggling to Afford New Equipment After NHS
    Budget Cuts," *The Guardian*, May 22, 2018, https://www.theguardian.com/
    society/2018/may/22/hospitals-struggling-to-afford-new-equipment-after-
    nhs-budget-cuts.

76 Campbell, "Hospitals Struggling."

77 Lesley Hannah, "Is the Current UK System of Pharmaceutical Price
    Regulation Working?," Hausfeld, February 14, 2017, https://www.hausfeld.
    com/news-press/is-the-current-uk-system-of-pharmaceutical-price-
    regulation-working.

78 Hannah, "Current UK System."

79 Badger, "Examination of International Drug Pricing Policies."

80 Badger, "Examination of International Drug Pricing Policies."

81 Badger, "Examination of International Drug Pricing Policies."

82 Joy Ogden, "QALYs and Their Role in the NICE Decision-Making Process," *Prescriber*, April 2017, https://onlinelibrary.wiley.com/doi/pdf/10.1002/psb.1562, p. 42.

83 Ogden, "QALYs and Their Role," p. 42.

84 Ogden, "QALYs and Their Role," p. 43.

85 Adapted from examples in Ogden, "QALYs and Their Role," p. 43.

86 Ogden, "QALYs and Their Role," p. 43.

87 Christina Walker, "My Son's Life Depends on This Cystic Fibrosis Drug: And Ministers Stand in the Way," *The Guardian*, February 4, 2019, https://www.theguardian.com/commentisfree/2019/feb/04/save-lives-cystic-fibrosis-orkambi-nhs.

88 "About Cystic Fibrosis," Cystic Fibrosis Foundation, https://www.cff.org/What-is-CF/About-Cystic-Fibrosis; "Cystic Fibrosis," Mayo Clinic, July 9, 2019, https://www.mayoclinic.org/diseases-conditions/cystic-fibrosis/symptoms-causes/syc-20353700.

89 Walker, "My Son's Life."

90 Walker, "My Son's Life."

91 "About Cystic Fibrosis."

92 "CF Foundation Celebrates FDA Approval of Orkambi as Important Advance for the CF Community," Cystic Fibrosis Foundation, July 2, 2015, https://www.cff.org/News/News-Archive/2015/CF-Foundation-Celebrates-FDA-Approval-of-Orkambi-as-Important-Advance-for-the-CF-Community.

93 Denise Roland, "Vertex Resolves Yearslong Drug-Price Dispute in England," *The Wall Street Journal*, October 24, 2019, https://www.wsj.com/articles/vertex-resolves-yearslong-drug-price-dispute-in-england-11571928563.

94 Sarah Boseley, "Calls for Action on Patients Denied £100,000 Cystic Fibrosis Drug," *The Guardian*, February 3, 2019, https://www.theguardian.com/science/2019/feb/03/nhs-cystic-fibrosis-drug-orkambi-vertex.

95 Katie Thomas, "A Drug Costs $272,000 a Year: Not So Fast, Says New York State," *New York Times*, June 24, 2018, https://www.nytimes.com/2018/06/24/health/drug-prices-orkambi-new-york.html.

96 Allie Nawrat, "NHS England Calls Vertex an 'Extreme Outlier' in Conduct of Orkambi Negotiations," Pharmaceutical Technology, March 7, 2019, https://www.pharmaceutical-technology.com/news/nhs-england-calls-vertex-an-extreme-outlier-in-conduct-of-orkambi-negotiations.

97 Roland, "Vertex Resolves Yearslong Drug-Price Dispute."

98 "Orkambi," Cystic Fibrosis Trust, accessed March 13, 2019, https://www.cysticfibrosis.org.uk/the-work-we-do/campaigning-hard/stopping-the-clock/orkambi.

99 Boseley, "Calls for Action."

100 Patrick Greenfield, "NHS Wields the Axe on 17 'Unnecessary Procedures,'" *The Guardian*, June 30, 2018, https://www.theguardian.com/society/2018/jun/29/nhs-wields-the-axe-on-17-unnecessary-procedures.

101 Laura Donnelly, "Prostate Cancer Victims Denied 'Game-Changing' Drug," *The Telegraph*, June 6, 2018, https://www.telegraph.co.uk/news/2018/06/06/prostate-cancer-victims-denied-game-changing-drug.

102 Donnelly, "Prostate Cancer Victims Denied."

103 "Can I Demand a Specific Treatment?," NHS, June 8, 2018, https://www.nhs.

uk/common-health-questions/nhs-services-and-treatments/can-i-demand-a-specific-treatment.

104 "Procedures of Limited Clinical Value," Ration Watch, accessed March 26, 2019, http://www.rationwatch.co.uk/ccgs; Campbell, "NHS England Restricts Patients' Access."

105 Campbell, "NHS England Restricts Patients' Access."

106 Denis Campbell and Pamela Duncan, "Long Delays to NHS Cataract Operations Leave Elderly at Risk," *The Guardian*, July 20, 2019, https://www.theguardian.com/society/2019/jul/20/massive-delays-in-cataract-operations-elderly-vulnerable-private-sector.

107 Campbell and Duncan, "Long Delays."

108 "Procedures of Limited Clinical Value."

109 Marcus Hughes, "Mum Denied Life-Saving Liver Transplant Describes Daily Struggle to Stay Strong for Her Family," WalesOnline, March 3, 2019, https://www.walesonline.co.uk/news/health/mum-denied-life-saving-liver-15908451.

110 Hughes, "Mum Denied Life-Saving Liver Transplant."

111 "Primary Biliary Cholangitis," Mayo Clinic, March 9, 2018, https://www.mayoclinic.org/diseases-conditions/primary-biliary-cholangitis-pbc/symptoms-causes/syc-20376874.

112 "Primary Biliary Cholangitis."

113 Marcus Hughes, "Grandmother Given Eight Months to Live After Being Refused Life-Saving Liver Transplant," WalesOnline, February 23, 2018, https://www.walesonline.co.uk/news/wales-news/grandmother-given-eight-months-live-14326248.

114 Hughes, "Grandmother Given Eight Months."

115 Hughes, "Grandmother Given Eight Months."

116 Marcus Hughes, "Single Mum 'Denied Life-Saving NHS Transplant After She Couldn't Afford Eight-Hour Round Trip to Hospital Appointments,'" *The Mirror*, February 24, 2018, https://www.mirror.co.uk/lifestyle/health/single-mum-denied-life-saving-12078979.

117 Hughes, "Single Mum Denied."

118 Hughes, "Single Mum Denied."

119 Hughes, "Grandmother Given Eight Months."

120 Hughes, "Mum Denied Life-Saving Liver Transplant."

121 Hughes, "Mum Denied Life-Saving Liver Transplant."

122 Hughes, "Grandmother Given Eight Months."

123 Hughes, "Single Mum Denied."

124 Gareth Iacobucci, "Surge in Exceptional Funding Requests," *BMJ* 358 (2017), https://www.bmj.com/bmj/section-pdf/947166?path=/bmj/358/8113/This_Week.full.pdf, p. 43.

125 Jon Ungoed-Thomas, "Doctors Warn NHS Is Rationing Best Drugs to Cut Costs," *The Times*, April 16, 2017, https://www.thetimes.co.uk/article/doctors-warn-nhs-is-rationing-best-drugs-to-cut-costs-l9cp6blgl.

CHAPTER SIX: THE HORRORS OF SINGLE-PAYER
INSURANCE—FINANCIAL COSTS

1 P.J. O'Rourke, "The Liberty Manifesto," Cato Institute, May 6, 1993, https://www.cato.org/publications/speeches/liberty-manifesto.

2   "Health Spending," OECD, 2019, https://data.oecd.org/healthres/health-spending.htm.

3   OECD, "Health Expenditure and Financing: Health Expenditure Indicators," OECD Health Statistics (database), accessed September 20, 2019, https://stats.oecd.org/viewhtml.aspx?datasetcode=SHA&lang=en#.

4   OECD, "Health Expenditure and Financing."

5   Anna Charles, Leo Ewbank, Helen McKenna, and Lillie Wenzel, "The NHS Long-Term Plan Explained," The King's Fund, January 23, 2019, https://www.kingsfund.org.uk/publications/nhs-long-term-plan-explained.

6   David Maddox, "NHS Crisis: Health Service in 'Perilous State' Warns Public Accounts Committee," Express, March 27, 2018, https://www.express.co.uk/news/politics/937352/NHS-crisis-Public-Accounts-Committee-warning-jeremy-hunt.

7   Sam Blanchard, "Theresa May's Promise of £20.5 Billion Funding Boost for the NHS Won't Even Be Enough to Cover Costs Let Alone Improve Patient Care, Think-Tank Report Warns," Daily Mail, December 17, 2018, https://www.dailymail.co.uk/health/article-6496053/Theresa-Mays-promise-20-5billion-funding-boost-NHS-wont-improve-care.html.

8   Bacchus Barua, Milagros Palacios, and Joel Emes, "The Sustainability of Health Care Spending in Canada 2017," Fraser Institute, March 14, 2017, https://www.fraserinstitute.org/studies/sustainability-of-health-care-spending-in-canada-2017.

9   OECD, "Health Expenditure and Financing."

10   "Health Spending," Canadian Institute for Health Information, accessed April 9, 2019, https://www.cihi.ca/en/health-spending.

11   Allin and Rudoler, "The Canadian Health Care System."

12   "Briefing Book: How Could We Improve the Federal Tax System?," Tax Policy Center, https://www.taxpolicycenter.org/briefing-book/what-vat.

13   "June 2016: VAT Rates Change in Canada," Insatax, June 2016, http://www.insatax.com/news/june-2016-vat-rates-change-canada.

14   "Income Tax Rates and Personal Allowances," U.K. Government, accessed April 26, 2019, https://www.gov.uk/income-tax-rates; Amir El-Sabaie, "2019 Tax Brackets," Tax Foundation, November 28, 2018, https://taxfoundation.org/2019-tax-brackets.

15   "Canadian Income Tax Rates for Individual—Current and Previous Years," Government of Canada, 2019, https://www.canada.ca/en/revenue-agency/services/tax/individuals/frequently-asked-questions-individuals/canadian-income-tax-rates-individuals-current-previous-years.html.

16   Morgan Scarboro, "State Individual Income Tax Rates and Brackets for 2018," Tax Foundation, March 5, 2018, https://taxfoundation.org/state-individual-income-tax-rates-brackets-2018.

17   "Briefing Book: How Do US Taxes Compare Internationally," Tax Policy Center, accessed April 25, 2019, https://www.taxpolicycenter.org/briefing-book/how-do-us-taxes-compare-internationally.

18   Milagros Palacios and Bacchus Barua, "The Price of Public Health Care Insurance, 2019," Fraser Institute, August 2019, https://www.fraserinstitute.org/sites/default/files/price-of-public-health-care-insurance-2019.pdf, p. 6.

19   Palacios and Barua, "The Price of Public Health Care Insurance," p. 7.

20 Palacios and Barua, "The Price of Public Health Care Insurance," p. 1.

21 Rachael Harker, "NHS Funding and Expenditure," U.K. Commons Briefing papers CBP0724, April 13, 2018, https://researchbriefings.files.parliament.uk/documents/SN00724/SN00724.pdf, p. 12.

22 Andrew Gregory, "Taxes Need to Be Hiked by £2,000 a Year Per Household to Save the NHS," *The Mirror*, May 24, 2018, https://www.mirror.co.uk/news/politics/taxes-need-hiked-2000-year-12586191.

23 $135,000 · 7,000 = 945 million; Papanicolas, Woskie, and Jha, "Health Care Spending"; The Health Foundation et al., *Closing the Gap*, p. 17.

24 Karen Motley, "NHS Offering £18,500 'Relocation Support' for UK-Qualified GPS," Chadwick Lawrence, March 22, 2019, http://www.chadwicklawrence.co.uk/legal-news/nhs-offering-18500-relocation-support-uk-qualified-gps.

25 Kisalaya Basu, Georgia Livadiotakis, and Serge Tanguay, "The Gridlock in Canadian Hospitals: Which Patients Are *Overstaying*, to What Extent, and Why?," Canadian Association for Health Services and Policy Conference, Toronto, ON, May 10–12, 2016, https://www.cahspr.ca/en/presentation/5750791c37dee8907f702e02, p. 19.

26 Graham Hicks, "Bed-Blockers Remain a Problem for Alberta Hospitals," *Edmonton Sun*, January 26, 2017, http://www.edmontonsun.com/2017/01/26/bed-blockers-remain-a-problem-for-alberta-hospitals.

27 Basu, Livadiotakis, and Tanguay, "The Gridlock in Canadian Hospitals."

28 Nick Triggle, "Fraud Could Be Costing NHS in England £5.7bn a Year, Says Report," BBC News, September 24, 2015, https://www.bbc.com/news/health-34326934.

29 Kate Pickles and Stephen Matthews, "NHS Trusts Are Spending MILLIONS to Replace Crutches, Walking Sticks and Wheelchairs That Are Never Returned, Investigation Reveals," *Daily Mail*, January 2, 2019, https://www.dailymail.co.uk/health/article-6545765/Revealed-The-NHS-trusts-spending-crutches-never-returned.html.

30 Rosie Taylor, Sophie Borland, and Brendan McFadden, "Revealed: NHS Spent More Than £3 Million on Toothpaste, Shampoo and Other Toiletries After a Rise in Prescriptions for Items Many Patients Buy Themselves," *Daily Mail*, July 30, 2018, https://www.dailymail.co.uk/news/article-6003991/NHS-spent-3million-toothpaste-shampoo-toiletries-prescription-rise.html.

31 Taylor, Borland, and McFadden, "Revealed: NHS."

32 "Health Expenditure and Financing," OECD, 2019, accessed September 20, 2019, http://stats.oecd.org/Index.aspx?DataSetCode=SHA#.

33 Stephen Adams and Jonathan Bucks, "Middle England's £623 Million Bailout for the NHS: Families Are Forced into Debt to Pay for Vital Surgery as the Waiting List Hits Four Million," *Daily Mail*, September 30, 2017, https://www.dailymail.co.uk/health/article-4937418/Middle-England-s-623million-bailout-NHS.html.

34 Sophie Borland, "Pay £15,000 to Jump the Queue for a Hip Operation on the NHS: Hospitals Encourage Patients to Self-Fund Knee Replacements and Cataracts Surgery," *Daily Mail*, July 21, 2018, https://www.dailymail.co.uk/news/article-5976551/Pay-15-000-jump-queue-hip-operation-NHS.html.

35 Allin and Rudoler, "The Canadian Health Care System"; Blue Cross, home page, http://www.bluecross.ca/en/index.html.

36 "Health Expenditure and Financing," accessed September 20, 2019.

37 Ashra Kolhatkar, Lucy Cheng, Steven G. Morgan, Laurie J. Goldsmith, Irfan A. Dhalla, Anne M. Holbrook, and Michael R. Law, "Patterns of Borrowing to Finance Out-of-Pocket Prescription Drug Costs in Canada: A Descriptive Analysis," *CMAJ Open* 6, no. 4 (November 19, 2018): E544–E550, http://cmajopen.ca/content/6/4/E544.full.

38 Canadian Constitution Foundation, "Constitution Day 2018," July 1, 2018, http://theccf.ca/wp-content/uploads/2018/03/2018-Constitution-Day-healthcare.pdf.

39 Craig, "The Flight of the Sick."

40 Amy Spencer, "Michael Bublé on Christmas Traditions, His Son's Battle with Liver Cancer & Spreading the Love with New Album," *Parade*, December 28, 2018, https://parade.com/725651/amyspencer/michael-buble-on-christmas-traditions-his-sons-battle-with-liver-cancer-spreading-the-love-with-new-album.

41 Spencer, "Michael Bublé."

42 Cydney Henderson, "Michael Buble Gets Emotional Talking About 5-Year-Old Son's Cancer Battle: 'I'm Not OK,'" *USA Today*, October 29, 2018, https://www.usatoday.com/story/life/people/2018/10/28/michael-buble-gets-emotional-talking-sons-battle-cancer/1801985002; "Best Children's Hospitals for Cancer," *U.S. News and World Report*, 2019, https://health.usnews.com/best-hospitals/pediatric-rankings/cancer.

43 Fiona Ward, "Michael Bublé Opens Up About Five-Year-Old Cancer-Free Son Noah: 'I've Been to Hell,'" *Hello!*, December 15, 2018, https://www.hellomagazine.com/celebrities/2018121565679/michael-buble-opens-up-about-son-cancer-free-noah.

44 Henderson, "Michael Buble Gets Emotional."

45 Sarah Boesveld, "'It's My Health, It's My Choice,' Danny Williams Says," *Globe and Mail*, May 1, 2018, https://www.theglobeandmail.com/news/politics/its-my-health-its-my-choice-danny-williams-says/article4311853.

46 Boesveld, "'It's My Health.'"

47 Boesveld, "'It's My Health.'"

48 Chloe Melas, "Mick Jagger Doing Well After Heart Valve Replacement," *CNN*, April 5, 2019, https://www.cnn.com/2019/04/05/entertainment/mick-jagger-recovering-heart-surgery/index.html.

49 Michael Chapman, "Chris Jagger: At Least Mick 'Has Not Got to Wait in Line for the NHS,'" CNSNews, April 8, 2019, https://www.cnsnews.com/blog/michael-w-chapman/chris-jagger-least-mick-has-not-got-wait-line-nhs.

50 "Apply for a Free European Health Insurance Card (EHIC)," NHS, August 28, 2019, https://www.nhs.uk/using-the-nhs/healthcare-abroad/apply-for-a-free-ehic-european-health-insurance-card.

51 "Health Services: Foreign Nationals: Written Questions—27365," U.K. Government, February 29, 2016, https://www.parliament.uk/business/publications/written-questions-answers-statements/written-question/Commons/2016-02-19/27365; Jason Farrell, "NHS 'Scandal' as UK Pays Millions to EU," Sky News, March 2, 2016, https://news.sky.com/story/nhs-scandal-as-uk-pays-millions-to-eu-10189381.

52 Bacchus Barua and David Jacques, "The Private Cost of Public Queues for

Medically Necessary Care, 2019," Fraser Institute, March 28, 2019, https://www.fraserinstitute.org/studies/private-cost-of-public-queues-for-medically-necessary-care-2019.

53 Joseph Brean, "Denied 'Assisted Life,' Chronically-Ill Ontario Man Is Offered Death Instead: Lawsuit," *National Post*, March 16, 2018, https://nationalpost.com/news/canada/denied-assisted-life-by-hospital-ontario-man-is-offered-death-instead-lawsuit.

54 "Ataxia," Mayo Clinic, March 8, 2018, https://www.mayoclinic.org/diseases-conditions/ataxia/symptoms-causes/syc-20355652; "'The Solution Is Assisted Life': Offered Death, Terminally Ill Ont. Man Files Lawsuit," CTV News, March 15, 2018, https://www.ctvnews.ca/health/the-solution-is-assisted-life-offered-death-terminally-ill-ont-man-files-lawsuit-1.3845190.

55 Foley v. Victoria Hospital et al., Ontario Superior Court, Statement of Claim file CV-18-00603786-0000, August 22, 2018, http://www.assistedlife.ca/superiorcourt-assistedlifecase.pdf.

56 "The Solution Is Assisted Life."

57 "The Solution Is Assisted Life."

58 Foley v. Victoria Hospital et al., Statement of Claim, p. 19.

59 Foley v. Victoria Hospital et al., Statement of Claim, p. 19.

60 Bradford Richardson, "Canada Denied Care for Terminal Patient, Offered Assisted Suicide: Lawsuit," *Washington Times*, March 19, 2018, https://www.washingtontimes.com/news/2018/mar/19/canada-denied-care-terminal-patient-offered-assist.

61 Avis Favaro and Elizabeth St. Philip, "Chronically Ill Man Releases Audio of Hospital Staff Offering Assisted Death," CTV News, August 2, 2018, https://www.ctvnews.ca/health/chronically-ill-man-releases-audio-of-hospital-staff-offering-assisted-death-1.4038841.

62 Favaro and St. Philip, "Chronically Ill Man Releases Audio."

63 Favaro and St. Philip, "Chronically Ill Man Releases Audio."

64 Steven Globerman, "Reducing Wait Times for Health Care: What Canada Can Learn from Theory and International Experience," Fraser Institute, October 2013, https://www.fraserinstitute.org/sites/default/files/reducing-wait-times-for-health-care.pdf, p. 59.

65 Globerman, "Reducing Wait Times," p. 60.

66 Barua and Jacques, *Waiting Your Turn*, p. 17.

67 "Absenteeism and Presenteeism Costs UK Workplaces up to £23 Billion per Year," BDA, June 2, 2016, https://www.bda.uk.com/news/view?id=123.

68 Shaun Wooller, "Clinical Negligence Payouts to NHS Patients Have Soared by £549 million in a Year to a Record High of £1.6 Billion," *The Sun*, July 14, 2018, https://www.thesun.co.uk/news/6776983/clinical-negligence-payouts-to-nhs-patients-have-soared-by-549million-in-a-year-to-a-record-high-of-1-6billion.

69 Stephen Adams, "NHS Hands Out £1million Payments to Patients It Has Harmed Almost Every Day as Big-Money Compensation Claims Rise 30 Per Cent in Two Years," *Daily Mail*, April 7, 2019, https://www.dailymail.co.uk/news/article-6894783/NHS-hands-1million-payments-patients-harmed-day.html.

70 Rajeev Syal and Denis Campbell, "Expect a Rise in Patients Suing NHS Over Long Waits, Watchdog Warns," *The Guardian*, March 22, 2019, https://www.

theguardian.com/society/2019/mar/22/patients-nhs-long-waiting-time-watchdog-national-audit-office.

71 Adams, "NHS Hands Out £1million Payments."

72 Wooller, "Clinical Negligence Payouts."

CHAPTER SEVEN: THE HORRORS
OF SINGLE-PAYER INSURANCE—OUTCOMES

1 Shaun Wooller, "One in Three NHS Staff Would Not Recommend Their Own Hospital to Loved Ones, a Survey Shows," *The Sun*, February 27, 2019, https://www.thesun.co.uk/news/8518837/nhs-staff-ashamed-hospitals.

2 Press Association, "Patient Safety Put at Risk Due to Lack of NHS Staff," *Daily Mail*, January 28, 2019, https://www.dailymail.co.uk/wires/pa/article-6640459/Patient-safety-risk-lack-NHS-staff.

3 Eric C. Schneider, Dana O. Sarnak, David Squires, Arnav Shah, and Michelle M. Doty, "Mirror, Mirror 2017: International Comparison Reflects Flaws and Opportunities for Better U.S. Health Care," Commonwealth Fund, July 2017, https://interactives.commonwealthfund.org/2017/july/mirror-mirror.

4 Selena Gonzales and Bradley Sawyer, "How Does Infant Mortality in the U.S. Compare to Other Countries?," Kaiser Family Foundation, July 7, 2017, https://www.healthsystemtracker.org/chart-collection/infant-mortality-u-s-compare-countries/#item-infant-mortality-higher-u-s-comparable-countries.

5 CIA, "Country Comparison: Infant Mortality Rate," *World Factbook*, accessed April 2, 2019, https://www.cia.gov/library/publications/the-world-factbook/rankorder/2091rank.html.

6 CIA, "Country Comparison: Life Expectancy at Birth," *World Factbook*, accessed April 2, 2019, https://www.cia.gov/library/publications/the-world-factbook/rankorder/2102rank.html.

7 World Health Organization, "The World Health Report 2000: Health Systems: Improving Performance, 2000, https://www.who.int/whr/2000/en/whr00_en.pdf, p. 200.

8 "Health Care System Performance Rankings," Commonwealth Fund, July 13, 2017, https://www.commonwealthfund.org/chart/2017/health-care-system-performance-rankings.

9 Korbin Liu, Marilyn Moon, Margaret Sulvetta, and Juhi Chawla, "International Infant Mortality Rankings: A Look Behind the Numbers," National Center for Biotechnology Information, Summer 1992, https://www.ncbi.nlm.nih.gov/pmc/articles/PMC4193257.

10 Gary Price and Tim Norbeck, "Infant Mortality Isn't a True Measure of a Successful Healthcare System," *Forbes*, April 12, 2016, https://www.forbes.com/sites/physiciansfoundation/2016/04/12/infant-mortality-not-a-true-measure-of-a-successful-health-care-system.

11 Wilco C. Graafmans, Jan-Hendrik Richardus, Alison Macfarlane, Marisa Rebagliato, Beatrice Blondel, S. Pauline Verloove-Vanhorick, and Johan P. Mackenbach, "Comparability of Published Perinatal Mortality Rates in Western Europe: The Quantitative Impact of Differences in Gestational Age and Birthweight Criteria," *British Journal of Obstetrics and Gynaecology* 108, no. 12 (December 2001): 1237–1245, https://doi.org/10.1016/S0306-5456(01)00291-1.

12 Christopher J. Conover, *American Health Economy Illustrated* (Washington,

D.C.: AEI Press, 2011), http://www.aei.org/wp-content/uploads/2014/06/-american-health-economy-illustrated_145021349951.pdf, pp. 256–257.

13 Associated Press, "Canadian Woman Delivers Identical Quadruplets," NBC News, August 16, 2007, http://www.nbcnews.com/id/20306323/ns/health-childrens_health/t/canadian-woman-delivers-identical-quadruplets.

14 Associated Press, "Canadian Woman."

15 Associated Press, "Canadian Woman."

16 Associated Press, "Quads' Birth Sparks Health Care Debate," *Billings Gazette*, September 1, 2007, https://billingsgazette.com/news/state-and-regional/montana/quads-birth-sparks-health-care-debate/article_4fd2209f-6d2f-5bf5-bcbc-5ee12979fca5.html.

17 "Timeline: Charlie Gard and His Parents' Legal Battle to Save Him," *The Guardian*, July 28, 2017, https://www.theguardian.com/uk-news/2017/jul/24/timeline-charlie-gard-and-his-parents-legal-battle-to-save-him.

18 "Charlie Gard: Pope and Trump Offer Parents Support," BBC News, July 3, 2017, https://www.bbc.com/news/uk-england-london-40479074; "Timeline: Charlie Gard."

19 NIH, "RRM2B-Related Mitochondrial DNA Depletion Syndrome, Encephalomyopathic Form with Renal Tubulopathy," Genetics Home Reference, accessed March 12, 2019, https://ghr.nlm.nih.gov/condition/rrm2b-related-mitochondrial-dna-depletion-syndrome-encephalomyopathic-form-with-renal-tubulopathy#diagnosis, "Diagnosis."

20 "Timeline: Charlie Gard"; "Charlie Gard: The Story of His Parents' Legal Fight," BBC News, July 27, 2017, https://www.bbc.com/news/health-40554462.

21 Dan Bilefsky, "Charlie Gard Dies, Leaving a Legacy of Thorny Ethical Questions," *New York Times*, July 28, 2017, https://www.nytimes.com/2017/07/28/world/europe/charlie-gard-dead.

22 "Parents of Charlie Gard Raise £1.2m for Pioneering Treatment," BBC News, April 2, 2017, https://www.bbc.com/news/uk-england-london-39471712.

23 "Timeline: Charlie Gard."

24 Children Act, 1989, c. 41 (U.K.).

25 "Timeline: Charlie Gard."

26 Bilefsky, "Charlie Gard Dies."

27 "Charlie Gard: Pope and Trump Offer Parents Support."

28 Lindsey Bever, "Charlie Gard Not Allowed to Receive Vatican's Care, Hospital Spokesman Says," *Washington Post*, July 5, 2017, https://www.washingtonpost.com/news/worldviews/wp/2017/07/05/charlie-gard-not-allowed-to-receive-vaticans-care-hospital-spokesman-says.

29 "Charlie Gard: Pope and Trump Offer Parents Support."

30 "Timeline: Charlie Gard."

31 "Who Was Alfie Evans and What Was the Row Over His Treatment?" BBC News, April 28, 2018, https://www.bbc.com/news/uk-england-merseyside-43754949.

32 "Alfie Evans: Legal Battle Toddler Dies," BBC News, April 28, 2018, https://www.bbc.com/news/uk-43933056; Patrick Sawer, "Alfie Evans Should Have Been Allowed Home to Die, Say Family's Supporters," *The Telegraph*, April 28, 2018, https://www.telegraph.co.uk/news/2018/04/28/alfie-evans-dies-long-running-legal-battle.

33 Jamie Grierson, "Alfie Evans Dies at Alder Hey Hospital After Life Support Withdrawn," *The Guardian*, April 28, 2018, https://www.theguardian.com/uk-news/2018/apr/28/alfie-evans-dies-after-withdrawal-of-life-support.

34 FBI, "2016 Crime in the United States: Murder," Uniform Crime Reporting, accessed April 2, 2019, https://ucr.fbi.gov/crime-in-the-u.s/2016/crime-in-the-u.s.-2016/topic-pages/murder.

35 "Intentional Homicides (per 100,000 People): United Kingdom," World Bank, accessed April 2, 2019, https://data.worldbank.org/indicator/VC.IHR. PSRC.P5?locations=GB; "Number, Rate and Percentage Changes in Rates of Homicide Victims," Statistics Canada, accessed April 2, 2019, https://www150. statcan.gc.ca/t1/tbl1/en/tv.action?pid=3510006801.

36 "Road Safety," World Health Organization, 2013, http://gamapserver.who.int/gho/interactive_charts/road_safety/road_traffic_deaths/atlas.html.

37 John Elflein, "Death Rate for Intentional Self-Harm (Suicide) in Canada from 2000 to 2017," Statista, August 9, 2019, https://www.statista.com/statistics/434539/death-rate-for-suicide-in-canada; "Suicide Rates," OECD, 2019, https://data.oecd.org/healthstat/suicide-rates.htm.

38 "World Drug Report 2017: Maps and Graphs," UNODC, 2017, http://www.unodc.org/wdr2017/en/maps-and-graphs.html, table 3.1.

39 "World Drug Report 2017," table 3.1

40 "Drug Overdose Deaths," Centers for Disease Control and Prevention, June 27, 2019, https://www.cdc.gov/drugoverdose/data/statedeaths.htm.

41 Laura Dwyer-Lindgren, Amelia Bertozzi-Villa, Rebecca W. Stubbs, et al., "Inequalities in Life Expectancy Among US Counties, 1980 to 2014: Temporal Trends and Key Drivers," *JAMA Internal Medicine* 177, no. 7 (2017): 1003–1011, https://doi.org/10.1001/jamainternmed.2017.0918; Richard Luscombe, "Life Expectancy Gap Between Rich and Poor US Regions Is 'More Than 20 Years,'" *The Guardian*, May 8, 2017, https://www.theguardian.com/inequality/2017/may/08/life-expectancy-gap-rich-poor-us-regions-more-than-20-years.

42 Robert L. Ohsfeldt and John E. Schneider, "The Business of Health: The Role of Competition, Markets, and Regulation," AEI Press, 2006, http://www.aei. org/wp-content/uploads/2014/03/-the-business-of-health_110115929760.pdf, pp. 21–22.

43 Glen Whitman, "WHO's Fooling Who? The World Health Organization's Problematic Ranking of Health Care Systems," Cato Institute, February 28, 2008, https://object.cato.org/sites/cato.org/files/pubs/pdf/bp101.pdf.

44 "Cancer Statistics for the UK," Cancer Research UK, accessed April 2, 2019, https://www.cancerresearchuk.org/health-professional/cancer-statistics-for-the-uk/mortality%20-%20heading-Zero.

45 Peter Lloyd, "Blundering Hospital Medics Who Failed to Spot Cancer in Patients Cost the NHS £46.9m in Compensation," *Daily Mail*, February 13, 2019, https://www.dailymail.co.uk/health/article-6700575/Blundering-hospital-medics-failed-spot-cancer-cost-NHS-46-9million-compensation.

46 Rebecca L. Siegel, Kimberly D. Miller, and Ahmedin Jemal, "Cancer Statistics, 2019," Wiley Online Library, January 8, 2019, https://onlinelibrary.wiley.com/doi/full/10.3322/caac.21551.

47 "Cancer Statistics for the UK"; Canadian Cancer Statistics Advisory

Committee, *Canadian Cancer Statistics 2018* (Toronto, ON: Canadian Cancer Society, 2018), http://www.cancer.ca/~/media/cancer.ca/CW/cancer%20 information/cancer%20101/Canadian%20cancer%20statistics/Canadian-Cancer-Statistics-2018-EN.pdf?la=en, p. 6: average of the decrease for males (32%) and females (17%).

48   White House, *Economic Report of the President*, March 2019, https://www. whitehouse.gov/wp-content/uploads/2019/03/ERP-2019.pdf, p. 214.

49   T. Philipson, M. Eber, D.N. Lakdawalla, M. Corral, R. Conti, and D.P. Goldman, "An Analysis of Whether Higher Health Care Spending in the United States Versus Europe Is 'Worth It' in the Case of Cancer," *Health Affairs* 31, no. 4 (April 2012): 667–675, https://doi.org/10.1377/ hlthaff.2011.1298.

50   "Inez Rudderham Has Cancer," GoFundMe, created July 17, 2018, https:// www.gofundme.com/inez-has-cancer; Ryan Flanagan, "Hear from the 'Hopeless, Overwhelmed, Scared' Cancer Patient Who Called Out the N.S. Premier," CTV News, April 30, 2019, https://www.ctvnews.ca/health/hear-from-the-hopeless-overwhelmed-scared-cancer-patient-who-called-out-the-n-s-premier-1.4402344.

51   Flanagan, "Hopeless, Overwhelmed, Scared."

52   Mairin Prentiss, "Cancer Survivor Who Dared Premier for Meeting in Viral Video Gets Her Wish," CBC News, April 30, 2019, https://www.cbc.ca/news/ canada/nova-scotia/cancer-survivor-nova-scotia-premier-1.5117479.

53   Jon Rumley, "Nova Scotia Cancer Patient's Video Plea Shines Light on 'Health-Care Crisis,'" *Huffington Post*, June 12, 2019, https://www. huffingtonpost.ca/2019/04/26/nova-scotia-cancer-video_a_23717905.

54   Rumley, "Nova Scotia Cancer Patient."

55   "Primary Health Care Providers, 2016," Statistics Canada, September 27, 2017, https://www150.statcan.gc.ca/n1/pub/82-625-x/2017001/article/54863-eng. htm.

56   Rumley, "Nova Scotia Cancer Patient."

57   Rumley, "Nova Scotia Cancer Patient."

58   Prentiss, "Cancer Survivor Who Dared Premier."

59   "Deaths from Cancer," OECD, 2019, https://data.oecd.org/healthstat/deaths-from-cancer.htm.

60   International Health Care System Profiles, "Breast Cancer Five-Year Survival Rate, 2008–2013," Commonwealth Fund, accessed April 2, 2019, https:// international.commonwealthfund.org/stats/breast_cancer_survival_rate.

61   World Health Organization, "Cancer Country Profiles: United States of America," 2014, https://www.who.int/cancer/country-profiles/usa_en.pdf; World Health Organization, "Cancer Country Profiles: United Kingdom," 2014, https://www.who.int/cancer/country-profiles/gbr_en.pdf; World Health Organization, "Cancer Country Profiles: Canada," 2014, https://www.who.int/ cancer/country-profiles/can_en.pdf.

62   Conover, *American Health Economy Illustrated*, pp. 258–259.

63   Julie Bosman, "Guiliani's Prostate Cancer Figure Is Disputed," *New York Times*, October 31, 2007, https://www.nytimes.com/2007/10/31/us/ politics/31prostate.html.

64   Bosman, "Guiliani's Prostate Cancer."

65 "Survival Rates for Prostate Cancer," American Cancer Society, February 7, 2019, https://www.cancer.org/cancer/prostate-cancer/detection-diagnosis-staging/survival-rates.

66 "Prostate Cancer Survival Statistics," Cancer Research UK, accessed April 29, 2019, https://www.cancerresearchuk.org/health-professional/cancer-statistics/statistics-by-cancer-type/prostate-cancer/survival.

67 "Colorectal Cancer: Statistics," ASCO, November 2018, https://www.cancer.net/cancer-types/colorectal-cancer/statistics.

68 "Colorectal Cancer: Statistics."

69 "What Should I Know About Screening?" Centers for Disease Control and Prevention, January 30, 2019, https://www.cdc.gov/cancer/colorectal/basic_info/screening.

70 "Overview: Bowel Cancer Screening," NHS, February 12, 2018, https://www.nhs.uk/conditions/bowel-cancer-screening.

71 "Cancer Survival Rates," Nuffield Trust, July 17, 2018, https://www.nuffieldtrust.org.uk/resource/cancer-survival-rates; "Colorectal Cancer: Statistics."

72 Bradley Sawyer and Daniel McDermott, "How Does the Quality of the U.S. Healthcare System Compare to Other Countries?" Kaiser Family Foundation, March 28, 2019, https://www.healthsystemtracker.org/chart-collection/quality-u-s-healthcare-system-compare-countries/#item-hospital-admission-rate-for-asthma-heart-failure-hypertension-and-diabetes-2015.

73 "Mortality After Hospital Admission for Acute Myocardial Infarction Per 100 Admissions, Patients Age 45 and Older, 2013," Commonwealth Fund, https://international.commonwealthfund.org/stats/mortality_myocardial_infarction.

74 White House, *Economic Report of the President*, p. 215.

75 Meera Baines, "'He Took His Last Breath in My Arms': Retired Kamloops Doctor Died in Hospital Waiting Room, Wife Says," CBC News, March 22, 2017, https://www.cbc.ca/news/canada/british-columbia/kamloops-doctor-dies-in-hospital-waiting-room-1.4035080.

76 Baines, "Retired Kamloops Doctor."

77 Letter from Janice Joneja to Minister of Health for British Columbia, March 18, 2017, https://www.documentcloud.org/documents/3521633-Janice-Joneja-Letter-to-BC-health-Mar-18.html.

78 Kendra Mangione, "'He Drew His Last Breath in My Arms': Widow on Doctor's Waiting Room Death," CTV News Vancouver, March 21, 2017, https://bc.ctvnews.ca/he-drew-his-last-breath-in-my-arms-widow-on-doctor-s-waiting-room-death-1.3335079.

79 Mangione, "Widow on Doctor's Waiting Room Death."

80 Mangione, "Widow on Doctor's Waiting Room Death."

81 Mangione, "Widow on Doctor's Waiting Room Death."

82 "Former NHS Director Dies After Operation Is Cancelled Four Times at Her Own Hospital," *Daily Mail*, March 31, 2011, https://www.dailymail.co.uk/news/article-1371861/NHS-director-dies-operation-cancelled-times-hospital.html.

83 "Former NHS Director Dies."

84 "Former NHS Hospital Director Died After Months of Abandoned Operations," *The Mirror*, January 12, 2012, https://www.mirror.co.uk/news/uk-news/former-nhs-hospital-director-died-119649.

85 "Former NHS Hospital Director Died."

86 "Former NHS Director Dies."

87 "Former NHS Director Dies."

88 Bacchus Barua and David Jacques, "Performance of Universal Health Care Countries, 2018," Fraser Institute, 2018, https://www.fraserinstitute. org/sites/default/files/comparing-performance-of-universal-health-care-countries-2018.pdf, pp. 30–31.

89 Barua and Jacques, "Performance of Universal Health Care Countries," p. 29.

90 Barua and Jacques, "Performance of Universal Health Care Countries," p. 31.

CHAPTER EIGHT: AN ALTERNATIVE VISION
FOR HEALTH CARE REFORM

1 Edward R. Berchick, Emily Hood, and Jessica C. Barnett, "Health Insurance Coverage in the United States: 2017," U.S. Census Bureau, September 2018, https://www.census.gov/content/dam/Census/library/publications/2018/demo/p60-264.pdf.

2 Joseph Antos and James C. Capretta, "Chasing Universal Coverage," AEI, April 10, 2019, http://www.aei.org/publication/chasing-universal-coverage.

3 Antos and Capretta, "Chasing Universal Coverage."

4 "Income, Poverty, and Health Insurance: 2017," U.S. Census Bureau, September 2018, https://www.census.gov/content/dam/Census/newsroom/press-kits/2018/iphi/presentation-overview.pdf.

5 Antos and Capretta, "Chasing Universal Coverage."

6 "Marketplace Average Benchmark Premiums."

7 Rachel Fehr, Cynthia Cox, and Larry Levitt, "Insurer Participation on ACA Marketplaces, 2014–2019," Kaiser Family Foundation, November 14, 2018, https://www.kff.org/health-reform/issue-brief/insurer-participation-on-aca-marketplaces-2014-2019.

8 "Briefing Book: How Does the Tax Exclusion for Employer-Sponsored Health Insurance Work?," Tax Policy Center, accessed April 17, 2019, https://www.taxpolicycenter.org/briefing-book/how-does-tax-exclusion-employer-sponsored-health-insurance-work.

9 Jay Shambaugh, Ryan Nunn, Patrick Liu, and Greg Nantz, "Thirteen Facts About Wage Growth," The Hamilton Project, September 2017, https://www.hamiltonproject.org/assets/files/thirteen_facts_wage_growth.pdf, p. iv.

10 "Historical," Centers for Medicare & Medicaid Services, December 11, 2018, https://www.cms.gov/Research-Statistics-Data-and-Systems/Statistics-Trends-and-Reports/NationalHealthExpendData/NationalHealthAccountsHistorical.html.

11 Peterson-Kaiser, "Out-of-Pocket Spending," Health System Tracker, accessed April 17, 2019, https://www.healthsystemtracker.org/indicator/access-affordability/out-of-pocket-spending.

12 "Publication 969 (2018), Health Savings Accounts and Other Tax-Favored Health Plans," IRS.gov, accessed September 19, 2019, https://www.irs.gov/publications/p969#en_US_2016_publink1000204081.

13 "IRS Announces 2019 HSA Contribution Limits," Plan Sponsor, May 14, 2018, https://www.plansponsor.com/irs-announces-2019-hsa-contribution-limits.

14 Michael F. Cannon, "Large HSAs Trump 'Obamacare-Lite' Tax Credits at Delivering Better Healthcare," *Forbes*, December 10, 2015, https://www.forbes.

com/sites/michaelcannon/2015/12/10/large-hsas-trump-obamacare-lite-tax-credits-at-delivering-better-health-care.

15 Ray Martin, "IRS Allows Higher Retirement Savings Account Limits for 2018," CBS News, October 24, 2017, https://www.cbsnews.com/news/irs-allows-higher-retirement-savings-account-limits-in-2018; Lorie Konish, "Here's How Much You Can Sock Away Toward Retirement in 2019," CNBC, November 1, 2018, https://www.cnbc.com/2018/11/01/heres-how-much-you-can-sock-away-toward-retirement-in-2019.html.

16 "State Insurance Mandates and the ACA Essential Benefits Provisions," National Conference of State Legislatures, April 12, 2018, http://www.ncsl.org/research/health/state-ins-mandates-and-aca-essential-benefits.

17 "State Insurance Mandates."

18 Victoria Craig Bunce and J.P. Wieske, "Health Insurance Mandates in the States 2009," Council for Affordable Health Insurance, 2009, https://www2.cbia.com/ieb/ag/CostOfCare/RisingCosts/CAHI_HealthInsuranceMandates2009.pdf.

19 Exec. Order No. 13813, 52 Fed. Reg. 48385 (Oct. 12, 2017), https://www.whitehouse.gov/presidential-actions/presidential-executive-order-promoting-healthcare-choice-competition-across-united-states.

20 Department of the Treasury, IRS, 26 C.F.R. 54, https://www.cms.gov/CCIIO/Resources/Files/Downloads/dwnlds/CMS-9924-F-STLDI-Final-Rule.pdf, p. 62.

21 "Retail Health Clinics: State Legislation and Laws," National Conference of State Legislatures, August 1, 2017, http://www.ncsl.org/research/health/retail-health-clinics-state-legislation-and-laws.aspx#Scope.

22 Sabrina J. Poon, Jeremiah D. Schuur, and Ateev Mehrotra, "Trends in Visits to Acute Care Venues for Treatment of Low-Acuity Conditions in the United States from 2008 to 2015," *JAMA Internal Medicine* 178, no. 10 (2018): 1342–1349, https://doi.org/10.1001/jamainternmed.2018.3205; Rod Moore, "For Better Business, Recreate the Urgency of Urgent Care," Athena Health, July 9, 2019, https://www.athenahealth.com/insight/better-business-recreate-urgency-urgent-care.

23 Eric Wicklund, "Telehealth May Save Money, but It's Not Yet a Necessity for Consumers," mHealth Intelligence, May 23, 2018, https://mhealthintelligence.com/news/telehealth-may-save-money-but-its-not-yet-a-necessity-for-consumers.

24 Michelle M. Mello, Amitabh Chandra, Atul A. Gawande, and David M. Studdert, "National Costs of the Medical Liability System," *Health Affairs* 29, no. 9 (September 2010), https://doi.org/10.1377/hlthaff.2009.0807; Lawrence J. McQuillan, "The Facts about Medical Malpractice Liability Costs," Independent Institute, October 1, 2018, http://www.independent.org/publications/article.asp?id=4634.

25 ASPE/DALTCP, *Addressing the New Health Care Crisis: Reforming the Medical Litigation System to Improve the Quality of Health Care* (Washington, D.C.: U.S. Department of Health and Human Services, March 2003), https://aspe.hhs.gov/system/files/pdf/72871/medliab.pdf, p. 39.

26 Marian Wang, "Insurers Denied Health Coverage to 1 in 7 People, Citing Pre-

Existing Conditions," ProPublica, October 13, 2010, https://www.propublica. org/article/insurers-denied-health-coverage-to-1-in-7-people-citing-pre-existing-condit.

27 Gary Claxton, Cynthia Cox, Anthony Damico, and Karen Pollitz, "Pre-existing Conditions and Medical Underwriting in the Individual Insurance Market Prior to the ACA," Kaiser Family Foundation, December 12, 2016, https://www.kff.org/health-reform/issue-brief/pre-existing-conditions-and-medical-underwriting-in-the-individual-insurance-market-prior-to-the-aca.

28 "Health Insurance Coverage of the Total Population," Kaiser Family Foundation, 2017, https://www.kff.org/other/state-indicator/total-populat ion/?currentTimeframe=0&selectedDistributions=medicaid--medicare--other-public&selectedRows=%7B"wrapups":%7B"united-states":%7B%7D%7-D%7D&sortModel=%7B"colId":"Location","sort":"asc"%7D; NHE Fact Sheet, Centers for Medicare & Medicaid Services, accessed April 17, 2019, https:// www.cms.gov/research-statistics-data-and-systems/statistics-trends-and-reports/nationalhealthexpenddata/nhe-fact-sheet.html.

29 "National Health Expenditure Data: Projected," Centers for Medicare & Medicaid Services, February 26, 2019, https://www.cms.gov/ research-statistics-data-and-systems/statistics-trends-and-reports/ nationalhealthexpenddata/nationalhealthaccountsprojected.html, table 3, "National Health Expenditures by Source of Funds."

30 "Data Bank—World Development Indicators," World Bank, accessed September 19, 2019, https://databank.worldbank.org/reports. aspx?source=2&series=SP.DYN.LE00.IN&country=.

31 Centers for Disease Control and Prevention, "Life Expectancy," National Center for Health Statistics, March 17, 2017, https://www.cdc.gov/nchs/ fastats/life-expectancy.htm.

32 Cristina Boccuti, Gretchen Jacobson, Kendal Orgera, and Tricia Neuman, "Medigap Enrollment and Consumer Protections Vary Across States," Kaiser Family Foundation, July 11, 2018, https://www.kff.org/medicare/issue-brief/ medigap-enrollment-and-consumer-protections-vary-across-states.

INDEX